THE POWER WITHIN

THE POWER WITHIN

A Psychic Healing Primer

ઐઅ

Dr. Rita Louise, ND

Cover Artwork:
The Dancer by Kim S. Lenz
http://www.viewlenz.com/

To order additional copies of this book, contact:

Contents

DEDICATION

This book is lovingly dedicated to my girl Kiko who validated that we are truly made up of innate energy.

I would also like to express a special thanks to Ruth and Shirl, who without their love and support, this book would never have been completed.

Introduction

Everyone has psychic abilities. There is a myth about being psychic that I would like to dispel right away. Being psychic is not about having some mysterious ability that you can only be born with or a genetic trait that is passed down one generation to another. In fact, we all have psychic experiences daily.

Most of us, we feel as if we have some level of intuition. What we have never been told is that being intuitive and being psychic are one and the same. Understand that the only difference between being psychic and using your intuition is the level of trust you have that your intuition is correct. Trust is the most important component when working with your psychic abilities. You must trust the information you receive from your feelings, your inner communication, the pictures that you see in your minds eye, or the simple and straightforward knowledge that what you are thinking is right.

It is through these abilities that makes working with your psychic energy is possible. Psychic healing refers to the ability to facilitate the releasing of stagnant life force energy from the physical, emotional and spiritual bodies. In essence, you are giving yourself or your client permission to let go of whatever energy they are holding onto. This energy can come from a multitude of places, from your childhood, your family or your job.

Energy that has been picked up and accumulated over time can manifest as a physical disease, however, even a small amount of stagnant energy can leave you feeling unbalanced or un-centered. It can leave you replaying a scene or incident over and over in your head. It can also manifest as an ache, a pain or feeling of being under pressure. These are just a few examples of how energy that has stagnated has taken away your ability of feeling at one with yourself. Being at one, right here, right now in present time, is your natural state of being. It is when your energy has stagnated that you are unable to be in that place of inner contentment.

There are two levels of psychic healing that we will be explored in this book, clairsentient (feeling energy) and clairvoyant (seeing energy). When working on clairsentient levels, you will learn how to feel the energy in your client's personal space, locating where the energy has stagnated and assist your client in moving it out. In turn, when working on clairvoyant levels, you will learn to look at your client's energy and identify what "pictures" or issue he or she is working on. Once this information is communicated to your client, you can then assisting in moving the unwanted energy out. There are many time when working on clairvoyant levels, that just the communication of what the picture or issue is enough to start the healing process.

I have found that in order to learn how to work on psychic levels it is easier to experience a tool or technique by utilizing it on yourself before using it with a client. For example, prior to working with the energy with your client's body, you will first delve into how energy moves and flows through your own body. This creates a first hand experience of what you are trying to achieve as well as a deeper understanding of what your client may be experiencing. Your personal experience validates you ability to create the same experience in your clients, while your clients experience will validate what you have just learned. They go hand in hand.

Looking at and working with psychic energy is a very simple thing to do once you understand how it works and have some tools to use. Your success and progress will be enormous. One of my early students had taken a couple of classes from me, learning some of the tools that are covered in this book. She started working with clients, and within 3 months was able to look at, work with and make communications about the energy she was seeing.

I've had another student that once she really understood the concept of Clairsentience, the ability to feel energy, she was well on her way to becoming a very competent psychic. All that she lacked was the understanding that all of the energies and emotions she had been feeling and experiencing all of her life were actually psychic experiences. Once she began to trust this energy, her whole life was transformed.

The key to working on psychic levels is Practice . . . Practice . . . Practice . . . . The more you practice on yourself, on friends, on family members and on clients, the more you will learn and understand the tool or concept being covered. In addition, each time you practice, you are giving yourself yet another opportunity to validate your experience. So don't just read this book. Live this book. Take the time to do all of the exercises, filling in the answers to the questions as you go along. It is the only way in which you will truly able to begin to trust in your own abilities.

My Story

When I was young, there was a TV show called the Sixth Sense. The show was about a psychic detective who solved crimes. During a typical episode, there would, of course, be a murder, and the psychic detective would be called in to help. When the detective entered the crime scene, he'd see images of the victim being murdered, or their ghost like image would be floating before him, where they'd provide him with a piece of evidence. Other times he'd pick up an item, like a piece of paper and have a precognitive flash where he'd see someone that was still alive driving their car off a cliff. This provided him with the opportunity to change the impending negative situation before it happened. As I watched this show, I thought this was cool. I wanted to be able to see images like that. I wanted to have precognitive flashes or be able to see events that had occurred in a room when I walked into it. I wanted to be able to touch an object and get information about it's owner.

From that point on, I started reading any books I could find on ESP, witchcraft (which was the only thing around in the 70s) and the paranormal. By the end of seventh grade, I knew I had some kind of psychic ability, but I didn't know how to tap into it on a regular basis. My expectation was to see things floating around, to have these "experiences". I figured that if I kept reading these books I would become "enlightened" eventually. By high school, I was introduced to my first deck of Tarot Cards and started reading for my friends and for myself. I thought for sure I would become psychic by doing this. **Wrong.**

Through the years I kept on trying, reading books on Astrology, Numerology, the Quabala (Jewish mysticism), personal growth, anything that would provide me with the information I'd need to finally become psychic. After 15 years of searching and studying, I found the Berkeley Psychic Institute, thinking, WOW, these people will teach me to be psychic.

My first validated clairsentient experience occurred while in a beginning healing class. We were learning how to clear stagnant energy from the aura (our personal space), practicing this technique on each other. That day, I happened to be working on the class instructor. Before we started, we were asked to pay close attention to anything that came to mind while we were doing the healing, and that we should mention it to the person we were working on. As I started working, I noticed a lot of energy sitting in her aura, on the back of her head. The next thing I knew, I was saying "bills, bills, bills". The class assistant looked at me and informed me that the instructor had finished paying bills just prior to class starting. I was really excited by this experience, but I didn't feel as if I were psychic yet.

Once done with the introductory classes, I immediately signed up and started in the clairvoyant program. The basis of the training was that you learned how to develop your clairvoyance by perform readings in a group situation, or as they called it, by "sitting in line" with one or more of the experienced readers. As my first real clairvoyant reading progressed, I closed my eyes as instructed, and waited to see these things float around the room. As you might imagine, this didn't happen.

A few weeks later, I went to my first psychic fairs held by the Berkeley Psychic Institute. I had only been in the clairvoyant program a short time and I knew I wasn't psychic yet. I wasn't sure what I was supposed to do there. I talked to the people at the information desk, told them I was a new student, and expressed my trepidation in performing readings. The gentleman at the desk looked at me and with a wave of his hand said, "Oh well, just make it up". Yeah right, I thought. They did, however, team me up with a more experienced psychic reader.

Our first client was a woman who had a question regarding her relationship with her husband. She was in the early stages of pregnancy, was concerned with what her husband thought or felt about her being pregnant and the pending child. I sat there quietly with my eyes closed. As the other psychic began speaking, in my mind's eye I was astonished because I was seeing everything she was talking about. After a while I started to share with the client what I was seeing. The information was in essence the same as the experienced reader sitting beside me, but it was from a different angle, from my perspective. When the reading was done, a light bulb went off in my head, "Oh . . . that's what they have been trying to teach us to do. I've been seeing pictures and images in my mind's eye my entire life."

The following week, back at the institute, I again sat in line, working at the school's weekly healing clinic. Since I was a new student, I sat way down the line, which was okay by me. I sat quietly as the more experienced readers worked with the clients. As the evening progressed, there was a client who owned a beauty parlor and leased out stalls to beauticians. She had come in because her business was failing. She could not keep beauticians, and was losing clientele. As the reading progressed, the more experienced readers spoke to her about contracts and agreements that she had in this lifetime and about the location of her shop.

For some reason, I was seeing something else. Scared, I meekly raised my hand, hoping to be called upon. When asked to speak, I asked the woman if she had a beautician with long red hair working for her and if she had left the shop angry. The woman replied that she did have such a person working there who recently quit. I communicated to her that the woman's anger energy was still in the shop, making it hard for others to come in. I proceeded to give her ex-employee a healing and also performed some healing work on her establishment, moving out the stagnant anger energy that was still in her shop.

When I finished, I opened my eyes and looked around. All heads were turned to me. I think they were as shocked as I was. From that point on, my comfort level and confidence in what I was seeing increased dramatically, especially with the newfound knowledge that I was indeed psychic. One thing that I quickly learned was that even though I may not understand what I was seeing, it must in some way make sense to the person receiving the communication. I had learned a new word. Validation.

It is never explained in any books on the market that this **is** the kind of "seeing" you want to experience when you are working on clairvoyant levels. It is in the mind's eye. This is where you see things "floating around the room" and this is where you see the aura. I was ecstatic and the first time this happens to you, you'll be ecstatic, too.

Before We Get Started

Validation

Learning to work with your psychic abilities is a very experiential thing. It is not something you can read about and then have the expectation that you will have these kinds of experiences. It is something that must be experienced first hand, validated, and then practiced and refined.

When you begin to tune into and listen to your intuitive or psychic information, you will find many instances where what you are seeing, sensing or feeling may seem crazy to your logical mind. This is a common occurrence. This is where your ability to trust the information you are receiving is the most critical. While the information may seem far out to you, as you communicate it to your client it will probably make perfect sense to him or her. This is called validation.

As you continue down this path, developing your abilities, validation is critical. Validation can come in many forms. It can be expressed through a simple shake of your client's head, where he or she agrees with what you are saying or even an outright statement that what you are sensing is true. Validation can even come in the form of a yawn or a sigh as you move stagnant energy out of your client's personal space. The key, however, is to acknowledge it that you have been validated. It is through validation that you will learn to trust our psychic abilities. So as you work with clients on psychic levels, don't judge the information you are receiving, just communicate it. You will be surprised at the amount of validation you will get.

Remember, being psychic is 10% ability and 90% validation.

Before leaving the topic of validation, lets take a moment to talk about it's nemesis . . . invalidation. Invalidation occurs when you say something to your client and then say **NO**. Invalidation is one of the hardest things to take as you are developing your abilities. As an energy worker, you will be learning to look at and manipulate energy. When you are working with a client, you will see or feel the energy in their personal space. Energy is neither good nor bad. It just is. There will be times when your interpretation of the energy you see or feel is not congruent with your client's life experience. In these instances, you may experience invalidation. There will also be other occasions, where your observation of your client's energy is correct. Your client, however, may not be in agreement to hearing or owning the picture or issue. This is called denial. When your client is in denial, you will invariably be invalidated.

As you work on yourself, or with a client, and you find yourself being validated, reach your right hand behind your left shoulder and pat yourself on the back. Congratulate yourself. Take joy in the moment. Have it increase the level of trust you have in yourself and your own abilities. If on the other hand you find yourself in a situation where you are being invalidated, say hello that the energy of invalidation and just let it go.

Intent

Working energetically is all based on intent. Intent can be achieved through the use of rituals. Rituals create a space and a mood to accentuate someone's intent. Let's take a look at the concept of rituals and intent for a moment.

In Native American tradition, the ritual burning of sage or sweet grass (smudging) is used to clear unwanted or negative energy from a place or an object. It is thought that the unwanted energies are carried out and away on the smoke that rises up, dissipating it into the atmosphere. When used with intent, smudging is an effective ritual. Instead, many people purchase sage, burn it and wave it in a room or on an object because someone told them it will clear the energy in a room. If these individuals perform the ritual without the intent that the smoke will move and clear the space, then little or nothing will happen. They are not working the energy.

There is a big difference between going through the motions and actually working the energy. Rituals are not required to produce results on energetic levels. You just need to imagine that things are moving with your thoughts and visualizations. Pretend that it is so, and so it will be. This is especially true when working with psychic tools.

Psychic Tools

In the physical world, when you want to create or modify things, you use tools. Carpenters use saws, hammers, screws and nails. Surgeons use scalpels, stethoscopes, x-rays and stitches. Chefs use knives, sauté pans, graters and spatulas.

When I speak of psychic tools, I am not referring to a divination tool such as tarot cards. Psychic tools, in my mind and in the framework of this book, do not exist in the physical world. They instead exist on the etheric plane, in the world of energy and intent. Like all things that exist on the etheric plane, they vibrate at a higher frequency than items on the physical plane. This allows you to create them in your mind's eye and use them.

Psychic tools are created and used through the use of visualization, postulation or pretending. All one needs to do is pretend they have a tool in hand and that they are using it to achieve a specific goal or task. As on the physical plane, so is it on the etheric. For example, when I want to "measure" energy, I will employ the use of a gauge. When I want to move energy that is in and around the body, I will cup my hands and pretend I am scooping the energy away. Sometimes, I will create a feather duster or a broom to do the same job.

Picking the right tool for the right job is important. Tools that work for me, tools that work within my frame of reference, may not be the same tools that will work for you. Throughout this book, we will be discussing and exploring a number of psychic tools. I would like to stress that it doesn't matter what kind of tools you use or what the tools looks like. This will not impact the work being done. They are just suggestions to provide you with ideas to try. Pick the tool, the visualization that works best for you. So if using Pam vegetable spray to make energy slide out of an aura works better for you than employing WD-40 oil, then go for it. The most important thing is for you to be comfortable and in your own integrity with the tools that you use. As we continue on, I am sure that this concept will become clearer to you.

Exercise: Your Reading Screen

Your Reading Screen is the tool you will use when working to develop your clairvoyant abilities. Your reading screen can be likened to a television set. It is the place you go when you visualize, where you see things in your mind's eye.

As you ask yourself questions, your reading screen will provide you with the answers in the form of a word, a color or a picture. Give yourself permission to receive a response to any given question. Trust the information you are getting. When you first start working with this tool, don't judge yourself or the information you are receiving. Also, it is not necessary to go into effort when trying to answer any given question. If you are not getting an answer quickly and effortlessly, just move on to the next question. As you get more comfortable with working with this technique, the answers will come. Don't worry . . .

Your reading screen should be maintained regularly. Many times, our reading screen can get dusty, covered with dirt or grime and even spider webs. Having a dirty reading screen, i.e. a reading screen covered with stagnant energy, makes it difficult for to see the information on it.

It is like looking through dirty windows or trying to watch a TV covered with grime.

To clean off your reading screen, create a psychic tool that seems appropriate. A feather duster or Windex window cleaner with a dry paper towel works wonders. Your reading screen has both a front and a back to it so make sure you clean off both sides.

To do this, ask yourself or the universe "can I see my reading screen".

Allow the image of this psychic tool to appear easily and effortlessly in your minds eye.

As this image appears, notice what does it looks like?

Is it clean and shiny or is it dusty and covered in spider webs?

Can you see its glass like surface or are there stains or even a layer of energy on the front of it blocking your view.

Take a moment to clean off your reading screen, both front and back.

How does your reading screen seem now? Can you see more clearly?

The Chakras And Psychic Abilities

The chakras are energy centers within the body. They are responsible for how you process information from your environment. They are also what allow you to have and utilize your psychic abilities.

There are seven major chakras within the physical body that run from the base of the spine to the top of the head. There are also chakras in the hands and feet as well as where meridian lines cross in the body as identified by acupuncture. Physiologically speaking, the major chakras are located where groups of nerves meet to form nerve centers. They are also related to the endocrine gland system, which includes the adrenal gland, thyroid and the pituitary gland.

The first chakra is located at the base of the spine near the tailbone. It controls your survival information, how you live and create or manifest things in the physical world. Think about a time or situation where you've been scared, hurt or your physical survival threatened. Do you remember experiencing a rush of adrenaline flowing through your body? In situations like this, the first chakra is responsible for processing your survival information. It opens, triggering the physiological responses needed, your "fight or flight" response. This chakra will return to its original size when the threatening situation has passed. It is also where you hold onto your fears, which can create anxiety or even indecisiveness in your daily life.

The second chakra is located just below the belly button. This chakra controls your ability to feel energy, which is called Clairsentience. Clairsentience is considered a psychic ability. The character Diana Troy on *Star Trek, the Next Generation*, for example, is Clairsentient. Diana feels things. When she communicates, she says things like "I feel" or "I am sensing".

We all have clairsentient experiences daily. Think about the times you have walked into a room and "felt" bad vibes, only to find out that an argument has just taken place. In turn, what about the times you've walked into a room that someone has just performed a healing or are deep in meditation. Does your body respond by allowing you to feel cleared and uplifted? You are processing that information through the second chakra. You are having a psychic experience. So when you are feeling energy or emotions from the world around you, validate that experience.

The third chakra is located just below the sternum. This chakra controls your power. It controls your ability to use your power or will for yourselves (will power). You also utilize this same energy with regards to others. You are experiencing your third chakra processing information when you get butterflies in your stomach, or when you "suck in your gut" and make a firm decision.

The fourth chakra is your heart center. Located in the center of the chest, it controls your ability to love yourselves and to love others unconditionally. This is where you store your emotions and build trust. Have you ever had the experience where you were asked to do something that didn't feel right to you? When you love yourself unconditionally, you can remain in integrity with yourself, making decisions based on **your** needs and desires as opposed to the needs and desires of others. The fourth chakra is a great place to validate your decisions. Try checking in on your fourth chakra to see if you get the warm and fuzzies. The warm and fuzzies are an easy way to validate that a decision is right for you.

The fifth chakra is located in the base of the throat, just below the voice box. This chakra controls your ability to hear information, which is called Clairaudience. Clairaudience is also a psychic ability. Do you think that your inner dialog is just your intellectual mind working overtime? What would you say if I told you the answer to that question is a definite **no!** You are always receiving information on clairaudient levels. You can be receiving this nonverbal information from your family, your friends and even from your spirit guides or angels. It can be experienced as a soft voice or a constant prompting to remind you of what your next step should be. You may even experience the workings of your fifth chakra as an outright answer to a specific question. This is your clairaudience at work.

The sixth chakra, or third eye is located in the center of your forehead, just above your eyes. The sixth chakra houses another of your psychic abilities, that of Clairvoyance. Clairvoyance is the ability to see pictures in your mind's eye. It is your ability to visualize, which should not be confused with your ability to trust or validate what you are seeing. Visualization is the most important tool you will use as you develop your clairvoyance. By working with your visualization skills, by flexing those visualization muscles, it will become easier for you to accept the information that comes in on psychic or clairvoyant levels.

Seeing clairvoyantly means that you see things in your mind's eye. As you continue to read this paragraph, can you picture or visualize what your house looks like or your car? Can you see your bedroom or your office at work? Can you see the vacation you took as a child or the face of your first love? Are you able to see all of these things in your mind's eye . . . clearly, easily, effortlessly? It is through visualization that you are able to see things on a clairvoyant levels.

The seventh chakra is located on the top of your head. It is through this chakra that you receive information and are connect to your higher self, the cosmic conscious, or God. The seventh chakra also seats the last of your psychic abilities called Knowingness. It is the ability to just know. When you work with information on knowingness levels, you don't know how you know something, you just do. Because the seventh chakra sits on the top of the head, the physical body and the other chakras may not have an opportunity to process the information involved. When you find yourself literally saying something right off the top of your head, this is your knowingness at work.

Below is a table that identifies the different types of information that is processed by each of our chakras.

Chakra/Location/Ability   Definition

First Chakra
Base of the spine, near the tailbone.

Survival	Your ability to take care of your body, i.e food, shelter. Houses your fears and insecurities.
Physical	How your physical body interfaces in the world. Health issues.

Second Chakra
Two fingers below the belly button.

Clairsentience	Your ability to "feel" energy.
Desires/Creativity	Your ability to feel your needs (including your sexual needs) and create for yourself.

Third Chakra
Below the ribcage.

Power, Energy	Your personal power, will power, drive, motivation.
Out of Body Experience	Your ability to dream, astral travel.
Out of Body Memory	Your memory of these events.

Fourth Chakra
The center of the chest, the heart center.

Affinity	Your ability to love yourself and others unconditionally.

Fifth Chakra
The cleft in the throat.

Clairaudience	Your ability to hear others, i.e. your Spirit Guides.
Inner Voice	Your ability to listen to your own information.
Telepathy	Your ability to communicate with others without speaking.
Pragmatic Intuition	Your ability to get from point A to point B and then to point C.

Sixth Chakra
Above the eyes on the forehead, the "third eye".

Clairvoyance	Your ability to see mental image pictures.
Abstract Intuition	Your ability to get from A to Z without going through all the steps.

Seventh Chakra
Top of the head.

Knowingness	Your ability to just "know".
Trance Mediumship/Body	Your ability to leave the body.
Trance Mediumship/Being	Your ability to allow another being into your body.

Chakras & Colors

There are many texts that ascribe a specific color to each chakra. Below is a list of the chakras and their assigned colors.

Chakra	Color
First	Red
Second	Orange
Third	Yellow
Fourth	Green
Fifth	Blue
Sixth	Indigo
Seventh	Purple

These colors are the **highest** energetic vibration that a chakra can obtain. These colors may be true but will **only** appear in the body of an individual who has **no** issues s/he is working on or processing. In my twenty years of experience, I have never met an individual whose chakras were so clear that all of the chakras appeared in those bright, solid hues.

The colors assigned to the chakras, however, are a great tool to use to clear and heal them. Let's explore this in the form of a meditation.

Exercise: Chakra Color Meditation

Starting at the base of your spine, locate your first chakra.

Breathe into the chakra, allowing it to fill up with red energy, moving out any other color or energy that may be present.

Allow that chakra to be filled with your highest vibration of red energy, washing away any fears, insecurities or doubts you may have.

Notice how good it feels to have it filled with energy that is vibrating at its highest potential.

Next, moving up your body, locate your second chakra.

The second chakra is located just below the belly button.

Find that chakra now.

Breathe into the chakra, filling it up with orange energy.

Watch as that chakra is filled with your highest vibration orange energy, bringing with it all of your creativity.

Notice how good it feels as you give your chakra a healing.

If you notice any discomfort in your body, say hello to that part of your body and as quickly as it came, let it go.

Continuing up your body to your solar plexus (just below the rib cage) and locate the third chakra.

Breathe into the chakra, allowing it to fill up with bright yellow energy and moving out unwanted colors or energies.

Feel the chakra being filled with yellow energy as you call back your power.

How does it feel to your body?

Next move on to your fourth chakra, or heart center.

Breathe into the chakra, allowing it to fill up with green energy, the energy of self-love.

Watch as your fourth chakra is filled with green energy.

Notice how good it feels to be able to love yourself unconditionally.

The fifth chakra, located at the cleft in the throat, vibrates at a blue color.

Fill the chakra up with blue energy, brining in the energy of your ability to communicate your thoughts, feelings and emotions.

Notice how good it feels to have it filled with that energy.

The sixth chakra or third eye is located on the forehead, just above the eyes.

It vibrates at an indigo color.

Breathe into the chakra. Watch as the clarity of your vision expands as you fill the chakra with indigo energy.

Notice how good it feels to have that energy radiating through this chakra.

Moving to the top of the head, the seventh chakra vibrates at a purple color.

Allow that chakra to be filled with purple energy, brining in with it all of your information.

Notice how good it feels to have that chakra filled with purple energy.

Now that you have filled all of your chakras allow the energy in each chakra to expand, filling your body with this wonderful healing energy, the energy of your highest good and potential.

Continue breathing into each chakra.

Notice how good this feels to your body.

When you feel full, vitalized and refreshed, stretch out your body, opening your eyes when you feel comfortable.

Now that you have completed this exercise, do you notice a change in your energy?

Do you feel as if you are vibrating at a higher frequency?

What else do you notice?

Working With The Energy In Our Bodies

Grounding

Grounding, our first psychic tool is a technique in which you can reconnect yourself to Mother Earth. As living beings, we tend to hold onto energy that doesn't belong to us, as if it were our own. By grounding you give yourself the opportunity to release unwanted or stagnant energy from your body, thus creating more space for you to be yourself. Grounding also brings you, as spirit, back into your body here on the physical plane. This will allow you to feel clearer, more balanced and in the present moment.

I consider grounding an essential tool for you to master. When you ground something, you are using your intent. To ground, you create a line of energy beginning at a specific point and have it travel down to the center of the planet. This is called a grounding cord. Then again with your intent, pretend that your grounding cord is releasing unwanted energy down to the center of the planet.

Your grounding cord can take on any shape or visual image that is comfortable to you. You can change the form your grounding cord takes at any time you like. Once you learn how to ground, practice creating new grounding cords as often as possible. Try grounding your body as you stand in line at the supermarket or while you are at work, creating a new grounding cord each time. It is an excellent way to quickly reduce stress from the body, especially if you are being affected by the world around you.

Grounding cords can be used to ground things other than your body. These include other people, animals, physical items, as well as concepts and ideas. When I first heard about the concept of grounding things other than myself, I thought it would be fun to experiment on my dog. My dog is slightly hyperactive, and it seemed like grounding was just what the doctor ordered. Unsure if it would even work, I gave my dog a grounding cord. The amazing and remarkable part of it was that she would literally stop, turn her head and look at me, shake her butt (knocking the grounding cord off) and continue running around as before. I found it very validating to see her stop and knock the grounding cord off.

Exercise: How to Create a Grounding Cord

To do this and all the exercises in this book, it is best to sit in a straight-backed chair, with your feet flat on the floor and your hands resting on your thighs with your palms up.

To create a ground cord, visualize a line of energy connecting your first chakra (the energy center located at the base of the spine) to the center of the planet. It is that easy. Here is a meditation that will help you experience grounding on a more profound level. You might want to try recording each exercise, speaking slowly, clearly and concisely. This will greatly assist you in achieving a greater depth to your meditative space.

To begin this meditation, close your eyes and take a deep breath.
Take a moment to notice what's happening around you.
Where are you in the room?
That's right.
In your mind's eye, look around and see what's with you in the room?
Orient yourself to your surroundings.
Say hello to your body.
Listen to your heart beat.

Breathe in again, and allow you, as spirit, to effortlessly rest back into your body.

Before we create a grounding cord, let's start by calling back your energy.

You can do this by visualizing a soap bubble or a big water balloon over your head.

Have it appear as a ball of golden white light.

As you call back your energy, this ball of golden white light is going to get bigger and bigger as it fills up with more and more your energy.

Where did you leave your energy today?

Is it still in your car?

Or did you leave some at home? Is it with a child or spouse who has something for you to do?

Or in a project at work? We often leave some of our life force energy in our jobs.

Maybe you went to the grocery store or the bank?

Think about where you left your energy and summon it back to you.

Give yourself permission to not know where you left some of your energy and summon that back as well.

Do this by drawing it in like a magnet. Allow your energy to drift into that water balloon, flowing into it and fill it up.

Go ahead and watch.

Notice how big that ball of energy gets.

Look at how much energy you left out there.

Think about how good it is going to feel when you get to have it back.

When the ball of golden white light is nice and big and you are ready to fill yourself up, go ahead and poke a hole in it.

Let your energy cascade over you.

You might find it flowing into you like water, like that water balloon just popped or that a magnet just released.

Allow all that energy to fill up every cell of your body.

Let that energy flow through the seventh chakra and swirl around inside your head.

You might feel it tingling or tickling a bit or you might feel a warm sensation.

Let that energy flow through you.

Have it come into your neck and shoulders.

Bring that energy into your torso and arms, filling them up.

Let it flow down into your ankles and feet.

Make sure that some of this energy flows down and around your back.

Take a deep breath.

You're doing a good job. You're giving your own energy back to your-self. That's where it belongs.

Take one more nice deep breath.

Now that you've brought in your own energy, it's time to create a grounding cord.

A grounding cord is a line of energy that runs from the first chakra down to the center of the planet.

The first Chakra is located at the base of the spine.

Put your energy and attention there.

You may find this chakra tingling, vibrating or feeling warmer as you put you concentrate on this area of your body.

Next, in your mind's eye, visualize the center of planet.

The center of the planet can look any way you want. It can appear as a hollow ball or a solid sphere. It can be made of molten rock or like the insides of a baseball. It can even appear as a ball of light.

Whatever you want the center of the planet to look like, have that appear in your mind's eye.

Now, create a line of energy that goes from the first chakra down to the center of the planet.

Let this line of energy appear as a Redwood tree.

Allow this Redwood tree to form easily and effortlessly.

When it reaches the center of the planet, allow your Redwood tree to form roots, hooking you firmly into the planet.

Imagine your body releasing energy down your grounding cord, your Redwood tree, all the way down to the center of the planet.

Notice how this feels to your body.

Did you notice any shifts in your energy?

Do you feel more relaxed with your grounding cord in place?

Do you feel more centered, clearer, or more at ease?

Continue to release energy down your grounding cord for one to two minutes.

Pause.

Now let's take a moment and call back some more of your energy.

Envision a new sphere of golden white light above your head and once again draw your energy back.

Watch as the sphere gets bigger and bigger over your head.

When you feel that your sphere of golden white light is full, reach up over your head and take hold of the sphere, bringing it down and around your body.

Notice how good it feels to bring this warm, revitalizing and healing energy down and around your body.

You may feel a tingling on your skin or the warmth of sitting in the amber glow of your own energy.

Take a deep breath and breath in some of this golden white light.

Allow it to radiate through your body, filling you with this wonderful healing energy, your energy.

Allow some of this energy to go down your grounding cord.

Notice how good it feels to be filled with your own energy again.

When your body feels full, vital and refreshed, stretch out your body, opening your eyes when you feel comfortable.

What did you notice as you made your first grounding cord?

Did you notice any shifts in your energy? What were they?

What did you notice as you filled your body with your own energy after you had grounded?

Exercise: Different Types Of Grounding Cords

Next we will experiment with creating grounding cords that have different appearances. Here are a few examples of grounding cords you can try. Use the previous instructions of how to create a grounding cord to make these new ones. As you form each new grounding cord, pretend that this grounding cord is releasing energy from your body. Notice how each grounding cord makes you and your body feel. Record your results after you try each one.

Laser beam:

Hollow tube or pipe:

Waterfall:

Greek or Roman Column:

Try creating a few grounding cords of your design. Record your results.
Type of grounding cord/How does it feel:

Type of grounding cord/How does it feel:

Type of grounding cord/How does it feel:

On a separate sheet of paper, draw a picture of your favorite grounding cord. Add some amusement to this exercise. Try using crayons or colored pencils when drawing this image. Why did you select this one over the others?

Exercise: Grounding Practice

Give yourself the opportunity to practice grounding as often as possible. As you practice grounding, record when and where you practiced. Also, record how you felt and if you notice any shifts in your energy when you did ground.

Location/Time: (example: supermarket; 2/3/00; 3pm)

Location/Time:

Location/Time:

Exercise: Grounding Other Things

You can ground anything by giving it a ground cord. By grounding a person, a place, an item, or a concept, you are providing an access way for stagnant energy to be released. Try grounding someone else, your pet, your computer, your home or office, or even a thought or concept.

What did you notice when you ground them? Record your observations.

Item: (example: Office at work; 3/1/00; 10am)

Item:

Item:

Item:

Item:

Your Sacred Space

Behind the third eye, your sixth chakra, in the center of your head is the hypothalamus. The hypothalamus controls the nervous system in your body. By calming the nervous system, the body naturally begins to relax. It also serves to eliminate the endless chatter that is goes on in your head. The easiest way I have found to soothe your nervous system is to create what I call your Sacred Space.

Your Sacred Space is where you can be at peace and neutrality within yourself. It can be visualized as a mountain retreat, a bungalow out on the woods, or even as a glass or crystal cathedral. In this next exercise, we will visit your Sacred Space. Allow your imagination to take you to the place that is yours alone and no one else's.

Exercise: Creating Your Sacred Space

Close your eyes.

To begin, let go of your old grounding cord and allow it to fall to the center of the planet.

Now, let's create a brand new one right here, right now, in present time.

Beginning at the base of your spine, at your first chakra release a new grounding cord that goes all the way down to the center of the planet, anchoring it firmly.

Check and see what you are using for a grounding cord this time.

Are you still using a Redwood Tree? Maybe it's time to try a new one.

Maybe a laser beam, or a waterfall or even a clear glass tube will work better for you this time.

It may also be time to make your grounding cord bigger, so imagine that the diameter of your grounding cord is growing, allowing you to release more energy from your body.

Take a deep breath.

Let your grounding cord do its job. You don't have to do anything. No effort. It just drains the energy out of you that you don't want.

Take this time to allow your body to release any unwanted energy.

You don't have to worry about what you have to get done right now. Let go of those problems you are trying to solve.

Notice if there is some pain or discomfort in your body.

Right now, at this moment, at this present time moment let it go.

That's right; drop it down your grounding. You don't need it.

In this moment, you don't have any problems; you're giving to yourself.

This is your time for you.

Bring your energy and attention to a point behind the third eye or sixth chakra.

This is where we are going to create your Sacred Space. Be in the center of your head right now.

Go ahead and be there. This is your place of peace and neutrality.

To create your Sacred Space, first visualize an indoor location.

Say hello to this space.

Is there a sofa, chair or ottoman in your space or is it filled with pillow and cushions?

Look around and see what is in your Sacred Space.

Is your space decorated?

What other kinds of furniture are in it? Perhaps a chair or some end tables?

Do you notice any knickknacks or trinkets lying around?

What color are the walls, floor and ceiling?

Does your space have windows and a door?

Is there a fireplace with a roaring fire in it or is the sun shinning in, filling your space with warmth and a golden light?

Say hello to your sacred space.

Pause.

Now, on the floor, in the far left hand corner of your Sacred Space, notice the trap door.

As easily as you saw the trap door, open it.

Create a grounding cord that goes from the trap door opening all the way down to the center of the planet.

You've just created a grounding cord for your Sacred Space.

Now that you know what your Sacred Space looks like, it is time to clean out any unwanted energy from it.

Pretend you are reaching into your back pocket and pulling out a large plastic trash bag.

Slowly and carefully look in each direction of your Sacred Space.

Do you see any papers, empty soda cans, fast food or candy wrappers lying around?

Place these items into the plastic trash bag.

Go around your Sacred Space and pick up Christmas wrapping paper, old toys or clothes that don't fit anymore and throw them into the bag.

Is your bag getting full?

When the trash bag is filled up, close it and toss it into the trap door and allow it to go down your grounding cord.

Reach into your back pocket and pull out a new trash bag.

Continue to go around your Sacred Space picking up any other trash you find, putting it in the bag, and when full, tossing the trash bag down your grounding cord.

As you work, you may also notice items given to you by other people.

If you don't want them in your space, throw them into the bag. It's up to you.

Again, check your bag to see if it's getting full.

Use as many bags as is required for you to pick up all the garbage, tossing the full bags into the trap door and down the grounding cord.

Notice how it feels to have all of the garbage picked up from your Sacred Space.

Take a deep breath.

Once the garbage is all picked up, reach into your back pocket and pull out a feather duster.

Go around the room and dust your space. Dust the walls, lamps, knick-knacks, and any furniture that is in your space.

If you would like, wash out your space with soap and water.

Polish the furniture with Pledge furniture polish, or clean the windows with Windex window cleaner.

It's your space and you have the right and ability to clean it in any way you want.

Create any tool that will assist you with this process.

Now that the walls and furniture in your space is sparkling clean, pull out a broom, and sweep the floor of your space, or use a vacuum cleaner.

Sweep the dust into the trap door and down the grounding cord.

How does your space feel now?

Does it feel cleaner, more refreshing?

Is it easier being in this space than it was before?

Go ahead and take another deep breath.

Take another moment to look around your Sacred Space.

Pause.

Do you have any company?

Say, "Hello, I see you", and then move them out of your head.

Show them the way to the trap door.

Ask them to leave or gently push them through and down your grounding cord.

Just do it.

No problems, no effort . . . this is your head.

Is your mother or father there?

What about sisters or brothers or close personal friends or business associates?

How about your dog, cat or other pet?

Carefully look around your room, behind the furniture, under knick-
knacks and even in the closet.

That's right, whoever you find; show them the way to the trap door.

Assure them that they will be okay and no harm will come to them, but
tell them this is your space and you are not interested in sharing it
with them.

Close the trap door and hang a "Do not enter" sign on it.

Take a deep breath and exhale.

Find a comfortable place to sit in your Sacred Space and look around.

You have created this space for yourself.

Notice how your body feels, now that you've cleaned out this space.

Does it feel as if there is more room for you to be in?

Enjoy being in this safe, Sacred Space for five minutes.

This is your Sacred Space.

Pause.

Before ending this exercise, lets take a moment to call back some more
energy.

Visualize a ball of golden while light over your head.

Summon your energy back from where you have left it in your past.

Call it back from the items or individuals you found in your Sacred
Space.

Watch as your energy comes back to you, causing the ball of golden
white light to get bigger.

Reach up and poke a hole in the sphere, allowing your energy to cascade down and around your body.

Pretend that you can breathe your energy in through your sixth chakra.

Notice how good if feels to have your own energy recharging your
Sacred Space.

When your body feels full, vital and refreshed, stretch out your body,
opening your eyes when you feel comfortable.

What did your Sacred Space look like?

What kind of things did you find in your Sacred Space?

Were there many people in your Sacred Space?

How did your body feel as you cleaned out your Sacred Space?

The Aura

The aura is the electromagnetic field around the body. It is your personal space. Clairvoyantly speaking, a healthy aura should appear like a giant egg or bubble that extend about 12-18 inches around our bodies. There are, however, seven separate and distinct layers in the aura. Each layer of the aura corresponds to a different energy vibration similar to that of the chakras, or energy centers within the body. Where the chakras process the information you receive from the world around you, the aura, in turn, holds onto the "pictures" or issues that you have experienced in your lifetime. You carry your pictures in your aura, so that you can look at or process them.

When you look through the different layers of your aura, you are looking through all of your accumulated pictures and issues. This is how you make decisions and have judgments. It is your accumulation of pictures that makes you the unique individual you are. It is these pictures you will learn to read as you continue to develop your psychic abilities. For now, however, you must become acquainted with your own aura.

It is easy to feel your own aura. First, rub your hands together briskly. Then, holding your hands about three feet apart with your palms facing each other, slowly bring your hands together. Notice if you feel any tingling, pressure or resistance on the palms of your hands. You may even experience your aura as a ball of energy between your hands. Continue bringing your hands together until they are about six to eight inches apart. Move your hands in and out until you can feel "the bounce" of your aura.

Practice this exercise until you can feel your own aura easily.

Exercise: Working With Your Aura

In this exercise you will learn how to manipulate your own aura. You will have the opportunity to feel what it is like to have your aura close to you as well as far away from your body.

Close your eyes and take a deep breath.

Say hello to your body.

Let go of your old grounding cord and create a new one in present time.

Go to your Sacred Space. Straighten up this space if required.

From your chair in your Sacred Space, notice your aura, the electro-magnetic field around your body.

Your aura should extend all the way around your body: in front of you, to the sides of you, all the way around your back and around and under your feet.

Feel the edges of the aura.

You might experience the edges of your aura as the place where your awareness of the world around you ends, or as an energy wall or barrier around you.

Notice how the edges of your aura feel to you.

Become aware of how big it is.

Pretend you can pull your aura in around your body, allowing your aura to get smaller and smaller.

Feel what it's like to have your aura get smaller.

If you notice any resistance to bringing your aura in, visualize this energy going down your grounding cord.

Give yourself permission to release it.

Continue to bring your aura in around your body until it is about three to four inches away.

Notice how it feels to have your aura, your personal space so close to your body.

Do you feel better or worse?

Does you feel safer or do you feel more insecure?

Do you feel as if you are more in control of your personal space or less?

What else do you notice as you sit with your aura this close to your body?

Pause.

Now release your aura from this position, and imagine your aura expanding, getting bigger and bigger.

Continue having your aura spread out more and more until your aura is as big as a city block or even the county.

How does it feel to have your aura, your personal space so far away from your body?

Do you notice any people in your aura?

Maybe can feel a car drive through it or children playing in it?

Does this feel better or worse to you?

Does this make your body feel safer or more insecure?

Are you more in control of your space or less?

Pause.

Finally, call your aura back in around your body.

Imagine that it is about 12-18" away from your body.

Take a moment to increase your grounding cord to include your entire aura.

Let your whole space be grounded.

Allow anything you want to release from your aura easily and effortlessly drop down your grounding cord.

Pause.

Now let's take a moment to give to yourselves by calling back your energy from wherever you left it.

Do this by calling all of your energy back into a ball of golden white light above your heads.

Where did you leave your energy?

Is it in the kitchen cooking dinner or in the yard, raking leaves?

What about with a friend who's in trouble? Did you leave any energy there?

Take this opportunity to call back all your energy from these places.

Watch as this energy streams back to you, filling your sphere of golden light.

Notice how it gets bigger and bigger as you call more and more of your energy back.

When you feel as if your ball of golden white light is full, imagine a hundred holes forming in it, and little droplets of your energy are raining down into your aura.

Notice how good it feels to have these warm droplets of your energy rain down, cleansing and washing your aura out, sending any remaining unwanted energy down your grounding cord.

Notice how it feels on your skin, cleansing it, your skin absorbing the energy, filling your body with your own life force.

Take a moment to sit and bask in your own energy.

When your body feels full, vital and refreshed, stretch out your body, opening your eyes when you feel comfortable.

How did it feel to have your aura only three to four inches away from your body?

How did it feel to have your aura as large as a city block or the county?

How did it feel when your aura about twelve to eighteen inches away from your body?

How did it feel once you grounded your aura?

What else did you notice?

Exercise: Feeling The Aura Of Others

Once you become familiar with what your aura feels like, you can move on and try to feel other people's auras. Here is a simple procedure that will assist you in feeling the aura of others. Record how their aura feels to you.

Note: Whenever I work with someone other than myself, I refer to him or her as clients. In this and other exercises, you will too.

First say hello to your body.
Let go of your old ground cord and create a new one in present time.
Make sure your grounding cord is firmly anchored into the planet.
Bring your energy and attention up to your Sacred Space.
Call your aura in and around your body, tucking it into your grounding
*   cord and setting it on release.*
Standing about six to eight feet away from your client, hold your hands
*   up, with your palms facing your client.*
Taking small steps, move your hands closer to your client until you
*   begin to feel a pressure or tingling on your hands.*
This sensation may be the similar to what you experienced as you felt
*   your own aura, but typically, everyone's aura feels different. Some*
*   may be solid and easy to feel, while others may be soft and subtle.*
Validate yourself when you have found their aura and thank your client
*   for helping you to achieve your psychic goals.*

Record what you experienced as you felt your client's aura.
Name:

Name:

Name:

Life Force Energy

We are all filled with life force energy. This energy flows through our bodies making us feel alive and vibrant. We have all experienced this feeling after exercising or dancing, sitting on the beach, by the ocean, or listening to a favorite piece of music. It is that wonderful feeling of being at peace and one with ourselves.

It is important that you keep your life force energy flowing. Running energy is a great way in which to give yourself, your body and your chakras a healing. When you don't, your life force energy can become stagnant or blocked, thus creating fear or judgment of yourselves and others. If left unchecked, stagnant life force energy can even manifest in the body as physical disease. As you learn to utilize your psychic abilities, it is even more important to keep your life force energy flowing because you do not want your own fears and judgments to interfere with these abilities.

Your **life force** energy flows in channels through your body like an electrical circuit. Think of these energy channels as garden hoses and your life force energy as water running though them.

Your **earth energy** flows through a channel that runs up from your feet and travels up through your legs, ending up in your first chakra. It is then released down your grounding cord.

Your **universal energy** flows in through the seventh chakra, down two channels that run on either side of the back of your spine to the first chakra. Once there, it will mix with your earth energy and proceed up the channels that lie on the inside of your spine and out of the seventh chakra.

You will then branch off some of this energy, running it down your arm channels and out your hands. This is your **healing energy**.

Earth Energy

In the following section, you will learn how to get your life force energy flowing. In addition, you will learn how to control the amount of energy you are bringing into your body by opening or closing your chakras. You will also learn how you can affect your space by working with color. By changing the color of the energy you are running, you can change the level in which you vibrate.

Exercise: Getting Your Earth Energy Flowing

Before beginning this exercise, you might try taking off your shoes, and flexing or massaging your feet. While this is not necessary, it may help you become more aware of where your feet chakra are as well as giving them a nice tune-up.

First close your eyes and say hello to your body.
Allow your old grounding cord to fall to the center of the planet. Take a moment to create a new one.
Bring your energy and attention to your Sacred Space. Be there now.
Pull your aura in until it is about twelve to eighteen inches away from your body and tuck it into your grounding cord.
Set your aura and grounding on release.
Be aware of your feet chakra, right there in the arch of each foot.
They may be tingling right now as you put your energy and attention on them.
Feel the energy of Mother Earth as it tickles the bottoms of your feet and your feet chakra.
Go ahead and open the chakra in your feet.
Do this like a camera lens opening and closing or the dimmer switch to a light.
Open up your feet chakra right now and feel the clean, fresh energy of Mother Earth come from deep within the planet right up into your feet.

Bring in this wonderful energy up from the earth, traveling past your feet and into your leg channels.

Your leg channels run from your feet chakra through your legs to the first chakra.

Think of your leg channels as garden hoses, and the earth energy as water.

Allow this energy to flow through your ankles and calves, over your knees and up your thighs, where it will come to your first chakra at the base of your spine.

You're probably feeling it right now as your earth energy runs through your leg channels, clearing out any stagnant energy that may be present.

Have your earth energy swirl around your first chakra, releasing it down your grounding cord.

Your earth energy is like an electrical circuit; bring up energy from deep within Mother Earth, up through the feet, ankles, calves, and thighs, to the first chakra and releasing it down your grounding cord back to Mother Earth.

Take a deep breath.

Enjoy your earth energy as it runs through your leg channels.

Pause.

Now open your feet chakra.

Watch, in your mind's eye, as these apertures open up, getting bigger and bigger until they are completely open; open to 100 %.

Feel the change as the amount of energy running through your leg channels increases.

How does it feel to have 100% of your earth energy running?

Do you feel more grounded, or does this make you uncomfortable?

Notice how this feels to your body.

Take a deep breath.

Now close your feet chakras down.

In your mind's eye, watch as your feet chakra get smaller, going from 100% to 90, to 80, to 70%, getting even smaller, to 50, to 30, all the way down to 10%.

Feel the change as the amount of energy running through your leg channels decreases.

How does it feel to have only 10% of your earth energy running?

How does this make your body feel? Better or worse?

Notice if it comfortable for you.

Does it feel too heavy or too light?

Take another deep breath.

Now, adjust your energy so that the amount of earth energy flowing through your legs is comfortable for you.

Let your body feel good with this.

Notice that it is validated. Bodies like earth energy.

Ask yourself "what percent of my earth energy am I running now?"

Give yourself permission to get an answer.

Take a moment now to call back more of your energy.

That's right, imagine you have a ball of golden white light over your head getting bigger and bigger as you call more and more of your energy back.

Think about how much energy you have released as you ran earth energy through your leg channels. Now it is time to replace those places with your energy.

Watch as that ball of light gets bigger and bigger.

When it is all filled up, reach up and pull it down and around your body, having it fill your entire aura.

Bring some of your energy in through your feet chakra and have it run through your leg channels, replacing all of the energy that you let go of.

Notice how good this feels.

Take a deep breath.

When your body feels full, vital and refreshed, stretch out your body, opening your eyes when you feel comfortable.

How does it feel to have your earth energy running?

What did you notice as you practiced this exercise?

How did it feel to have your feet chakra open to 100%?

How did it feel to have your feet chakra open to 10%?

To what percent did you adjust your feet chakra to reach your personal comfort level? How did this feel?

Exercise: Working With Earth Energy Color

You can also affect the vibration of your earth energy by changing its color. Try this next exercise and record your results.

To begin, take a deep breath.
Drop your old grounding cord and create a new one in present time.
Check that your aura is around your body and tucked into your grounding cord.
Bring your energy and attention up to your sixth chakra and go to your Sacred Space.
Bring clean and fresh energy up from Mother Earth up through the feet, calves, knees, and thighs and into the first chakra, releasing it down your grounding cord.
Open or close your feet chakra to a percentage comfortable for you.
Enjoy it as this energy cleanses out your leg channels.
Breathe in deeply once again and exhale.
Picture that the energy you are bringing up from Mother Earth is:

Green. How does this color make your body feel?

Purple. How does this color make your body feel?

Orange. How does this color make your body feel?

Red. How does this color make your body feel?

Brown. How does this color make your body feel?

Black. How does this color make your body feel?

Select a few colors of your own and record how these colors make you feel.
Color/How does it feel:

Color/How does it feel:

Color/How does it feel:

Universal Energy

Our universal energy is energy that we run from the seventh chakra **through** the body **to** the first chakra. This differs from earth energy where you brought in energy from Mother Earth through the leg channels. Here you will be drawing in energy from out in the universe through the seventh chakra and bringing it down the back of the spine to the first chakra. You will then complete the "electrical circuit" by brining energy up the front of the spine from the first chakra back to the seventh chakra and out the top of the head. This is a wonderful technique you can use to give your body and chakras a healing. So close your eyes and get comfortable in your chair. Here we go with a new exercise.

Exercise: Getting Your Universal Energy Flowing

Say hello to your old grounding cord and drop it down to the center of the planet, creating a new one in present time.

Check to see that your aura is around your body and tucked into your grounding cord.

Imagine that your grounding and your aura are releasing energy.

Bring your energy and attention up to your sixth chakra and go into your Sacred Space.

Reach down into the planet and bring clean, fresh energy up from Mother Earth.

Bring it up through the feet, calves, knees, and thighs and into the first chakra.

Allow this energy to be released down your grounding cord.

Take a nice deep breath.

From the center of your head, notice each of your chakras: the first, the second and third, saying hello to the fourth, the fifth, the sixth and finally the seventh chakra.

Pretend that you are reaching out far into the galaxy, bringing a bit of the universe's energy back with you to the top of your head.

You are probably already feeling this energy on the top of your head, tickling your seventh chakra.

Open the seventh chakra and call in some universal energy.

Bring it down through your seventh chakra and have it flow down your back channels.

The back channels run along either side of the spine starting at the top of the head, at the seventh chakra, and continue down to the first chakra, at the base of the spine.

Say hello to this energy and experience it as it runs down the back of your head and continues down your neck.

Bring it down further into the body, through the chest, vertebrae by vertebrae, continuing through the back channels of the abdomen and lower back until it mixes with your earth energy in your first chakra.

As it is flowing through your body, allow it to fill and clear the back of each chakra.

Have your universal energy swirl around and mix with the earth energy in your first chakra for a moment.

Imagine a combination of your universal energy and your earth energy flowing up the front channels, which lie on the front of your spinal column, releasing the remainder of your universal energy down your grounding cord.

Bring some of this fresh, clean mixture up the abdomen and through the chest.

Continue up the front channels through the neck and head and up to your seventh chakra.

Allow your universal energy to flowing freely out the seventh chakra.

Imagine that it is fountaining out of your seventh chakra, filling your aura.

Watch it as it washes through your aura, cleansing it, and is finally released down your ground cord.

Allow this energy to fill and clear the front of each chakra as it flows through your front channels.

Again, take a nice deep breath.

Now that your universal energy is flowing freely out of your seventh chakra, allow about 30% of this mixture to branch out of the fourth chakra, the heart center.

This is your healing energy.

Have this energy flow up to your shoulders, down the upper arms, through *the elbows, down the forearms and out the hand chakras, clearing out any stagnant energy it may encounter in your arm channels.*

You probably can feel your hands warming up as your healing energy flows through your arm channels.

Take a deep breath and enjoy the feeling of having your energy flowing through your body.

Pause.

Now, slowly open your seventh chakra to 100 %.

Feel the change in the amount of energy running through your back channels.

Do you feel more present, more centered, or does this make you uncomfortable and spacey?

Notice how this feels to your body.

Take a deep breath.

Now close your seventh chakras down to 10%.

Feel the change in the amount of energy running through your back channels.

How does this make your body feel? Better or worse?

Open or close your seventh chakra to a percentage comfortable for you.

Take a deep breath and release it.

Watch your energy running through your body. Enjoy it.

Notice how effortlessly this happens. You don't have to do anything . . . it just flows.

Good job.

As your energy is flowing, take a moment to notice if you feel a cold area, a hot spot, or maybe some pain or discomfort in your body.

This is a block of energy.

Notice these spots right now and let your universal and earth energy heal and release these blocks.

Allow it to flow, to clean out and drain this energy down your grounding cord, so that everything is moving and flowing.

This is the natural state of your energy flowing and moving through your body.

Allow your energy to flow for a few minutes, releasing any blocks that do not belong to you.

Remember, running energy is only for you. It is not for solving everything, it's for you to say hello to yourself.

Take another deep breath and enjoy the feeling of having your own life force energy flowing for five to fifteen minutes.

Pause.

Now, let's take a moment to call back some of your energy.

Imagine you have a ball of golden white light over your head growing larger as you call more of your energy back.

Think about how much energy you have released as you ran universal energy through your back channels. Now it is time to replace those places with your energy.

Watch as that ball of light gets bigger and bigger.

When it is all filled up, reach up and pull it down and around your body, filling your aura.

Open up your seventh chakra and allow some of this energy to flow down your back channels.

Have this energy expand through your body, filling your body with the warmth of your own energy.

Notice how good this feels.

Take a deep breath.

When your body feels full, vital and refreshed, stretch out your body, opening your eyes when you feel comfortable.

How does this make your body feel?

How did it feel to have your seventh chakra opened to 100%?

How did it feel to have your seventh chakra opened to 10%?

To what percent did you adjust your seventh chakra to reach your personal comfort level? How did this feel?

What else did you notice as you had your life force energy flowing?

Exercise: Working With Universal Energy Color

Again, let's try changing your energetic vibration by changing the color of energy that you run through your back channels. Don't forget to record your results.

Drop your old grounding cord and create a new one in present time.
Check that your aura is around your body and tucked into your grounding cord.
Bring your energy and attention up to your sixth chakra and go to your Sacred Space.
Bring clean and fresh energy up from Mother Earth through the feet, calves, knees and thighs and into the first chakra, releasing it down your grounding cord.
Open or close your feet chakra to a percentage comfortable for you.
Enjoy it as this energy cleanses out your leg channels.
Take a deep breath.
Open the seventh chakra and call in some universal energy.
Bring it down to your seventh chakra and have it flow through your back channels starting at the top of your head, running along either side of the spine continuing down to the first chakra.
Using a mixture of universal energy and earth energy, bring this combined energy up the front channels.
Let it spout out of your seventh chakra and into your aura.
Don't forget to branch off about 30% of this mixture at the fourth chakra, the heart center, and have it flow up to the shoulders, through the arms and out the hand chakras.

Open or close your seventh chakra to a size that is comfortable for you.
Take a deep breath.
Let your body feel good with this.
Imagine that the energy you are bringing in from the universe is:

Green. How does this color make your body feel?

Purple. How does this color make your body feel?

Orange. How does this color make your body feel?

Red. How does this color make your body feel?

Gold. How does this color make your body feel?

Black. How does this color make your body feel?

Select a few colors of your own and record how these colors make you
feel.
Color/How does it feel:

Color/How does it feel:

Color/How does it feel:

Working With Energy On Clairsentient Levels

Clairsentience

In the first section, you became acquainted with your own energy, learning how to get it moving and flowing in your body. You experienced this by learning how to ground your body and by allowing your earth, universal and healing energies to flow. In this next section, you will learn to how develop your Clairsentience.

Clairsentience is the ability to feel energy. When you feel the "vibes" in a room, you are *feeling* the emotional energy in a location. This is one way in which you use your clairsentience. Many people experience their clairsentience when they "pick up" or sense someone else's feelings. You can also use this ability to feel the energy in your physical body, your chakras and your aura. You have already experienced using your clairsentience when you acknowledged what you were feeling, as you learned how to run energy in your body.

In this section, you will be utilizing energetic healing as the framework in which to work. I find it to be the simplest way to access and validate your clairsentience. Using your hands as receivers, you will learn to find, feel and clear your, and your client's space of stagnant energy. As you practice these exercises and explore the concepts presented you will begin to trust and validate that the feelings you have and are receiving are true

To explore these concepts further, you will first learn to perform each technique on yourself. By focusing your attention on *working with* the energy in your aura, chakras and physical body, you will get first hand practical experience. You will then build on that understanding by working and practicing on someone else, your client.

Aura Healing

Running energy is a technique in which to keep the energy moving and flowing through your body. But what do you do if energy has stagnated in your aura? In this next exercise, you will explore a way in which to remove this energy from your personal space.

Exercise: Simple Aura Self-Healing

To begin, close your eyes and say hello to your body.

Drop your old grounding cord down to the center of the planet and create a new one in present time.

Set your grounding cord on release.

Bring your energy and attention to you Sacred Space, clearing your Sacred Space as required.

Next, pull in your aura until it is 12-18 inches away from your body and tuck it into your grounding cord.

Set your aura on release.

Open your feet chakra and bring clean and refreshing energy up from Mother Earth, bringing it in through your feet and ankles, up your calves and thighs and into your first chakra.

Release your earth energy down your grounding cord.

Now, reach out far into the universe and bring some universal energy down.

Bring it into your body via the seventh chakra and have it flow down the back channels, vertebrae by vertebrae, until it reaches your first chakra, where it will whirl around, mixing with your earth energy.

Using universal energy and earth energy, bring this mixture up the front channels and let it spout out the top of your head, filling your aura with your own life force energy.

At your fourth chakra, the heart center, split off about 30% of this energy and run your healing energy down your arm channels and out of your hands.

Take a moment to sit and enjoy your own life force energy flowing.

Notice how good it feels to your body.

Take a deep breath.

Next, hold up your right or left hand physically in front of you, fingers open, palm facing forward.

Imagine you are creating a squeegee and holding it in your hand.

Notice how tangible the squeegee feels.

The squeegee is the psychic tool we are going to utilize to clean out your aura. You created this tool by using your intent.

Starting at the top of your head, at the seventh chakra, and going down to where your aura connects with your grounding cord, use your squeegee to smooth out your aura.

Do you notice any roughness in your aura as you work your way around your body?

This is where energy has stagnated or is stuck in your aura.

Say hello to that energy and watch it as it goes down your grounding cord.

Work your way all the way around your body, allowing all of the energy that is built up in your aura to be released and sent down your grounding cord.

Don't forget to clear the area behind your back and around your feet.

Notice how good it feels to have your aura cleared of stagnant energy.

Breath in deeply.

Do you feel as if you have more room to be yourself?

Do you feel clearer? More present?

Now let's take an opportunity to replace some of the energy you have just moved out of your aura by filling it in with some of your own energy.

You can do this by creating a sphere of golden white light above your head, and imagining that it will be filled up with the energy of your highest good and healing.

Watch as the ball of light gets bigger and bigger as you call back more and more of your energy.

Now reach up and poke a hole into that ball of golden white light, allowing all the energy you just collected to flow into your aura, filling up your aura with the energy of your highest good and healing.

Also, allow some of this energy to flow into your seventh chakra, down your back channels and release it down your grounding cord.

Notice how good this feels to your body as you give to yourself this way.

Take a deep breath.

When your body feels full, vital and refreshed, stretch out your body, opening your eyes when you feel comfortable.

What did you notice as you healed your aura?

How does it feel to have it free of unwanted energy?

Are there any other psychic tools that may feel more appropriate to you as you practice this exercise? What would they be?

Exercise: Aura Fluffing

As you have already experienced while clearing your own aura, aura fluffing is a great tool to use when you want to facilitate the releasing of unwanted or stagnant energy from someone else's aura. Now you will have the opportunity to take what you have just experienced and apply it to someone else. Working on others is a great way in which to validate what you are doing.

To do this exercise, you will need to have someone who is interested in having you work on them, whom I will refer to as a client. Have your client sit in a straight-backed chair, feet flat on the floor, palms facing up.

When doing any kind of healing work, it is also very important that you ask for permission before proceeding. Since you are working with someone else's energy, they may not be agreeable to you changing it. So please always ask for permission before you

As I demonstrate this and all of the other techniques in this book, I will be working on female clients. This is not meant to be politically incorrect, but does allow for the integrity of the book.

Before you begin, it is best to prepare yourself and your energy prior to doing any kind of psychic reading, healing or energy work.

To begin, create a new grounding cord and anchor it firmly to the center of the planet.

Say hello to your body.

Go to your Sacred Space.

Center yourself as spirit there.

Take a deep breath.

Bring your aura in and around your body.

Make sure it is tucked into your grounding cord and that your grounding cord and your aura are both set on release.

Allow your earth and universal life force energy to start flowing, remembering to send your healing energy through your arm channels and out your hands.

Take one more deep breath.

You are now ready to begin working on your client.

Start by having your client sit in a straight-backed chair, feet flat on the floor, hands resting on their thighs, palms up.

Before beginning any type of energy work, it is very important that you ask for your client's permission.

Ask "Would you like a healing?" If she says "Yes", continue.

Begin by creating a grounding cord for your client.

Her grounding cord should go from her first chakra all the way down to the center of the planet.

It is easiest to do this by resting your hands on your client's shoulders, and visualizing that you are creating a grounding cord for her, just as you have created grounding cords for yourself.

Once her grounding cord is in place, imagine that the grounding cord is doing its job. It is draining unwanted energy from the body.

Take a few steps back, till you are standing six to eight feet away from your client.

Rub your hands together to stimulate your hand chakras.

Raise your arms, palms facing your client and find the outside edge of her aura.

You may experience this as a change in temperature, a slight pressure, or tingling on the palms of your hands.

Once you have found her aura, pretend you can bring her aura in, till is about 12-18 inches away from her body.

Use your hands and feel her aura as you move it to the desired size.

Do this as simply and as easily as you have learned to bring your own aura in.

Also image tucking her aura firmly into her grounding cord.

Doing an aura fluff is similar to doing an aura healing.

I like to think of doing an aura healing as kind of like icing a cake, moving the energy in the aura until it is smooth and evenly distributed around the body.

Starting at the top of your client's head, work your way down and around her body. Move out any energy that does not belong to her.

Use your hands to move the energy or the squeegee we utilized earlier.

Make sure you work your way all around her body.

Don't forget to clear out the lower part of her aura, especially around her feet and where her aura connects to her grounding cord.

When you are done, call back some of her energy into a sphere of golden white light.

Imagine a ball of light forming over her head.

When it feels full to you, bring the ball of golden white light down and around her body, filling her up with her own fresh, healing energy.

Take a step back away from your client.

Inhale deeply and allow any of your client's energy to quickly and easily be released down your grounding cord.
You've just done an aura fluff!

How did you experience your client's aura? Did you feel a change in temperature, a slight pressure or tingling on the palms of your hands?

How far away from the body was your client's aura?

What else did you notice as you fluffed your client's aura?

Now take a moment and ask your client the following questions. It is through feedback from your clients that you will get validated for the work you have just done. Ask your client:

How do you feel now? Do you feel clearer, more present or relaxed? Could you feel my energy as I worked on you?

What else did you notice as I fluffed your aura?

You might feel a bit awkward using this technique at first, but give it a chance. In time, I'm sure you will come to enjoy it.

Lumps, Bumps, Whacks, Dents And Holes

When an aura is moving and flowing, it gives the

appearance of being smooth and shiny like a luminous egg. As you get more experienced in doing aura healings, you may start to find what are called lumps, bumps, dents, whacks or even holes in the aura. For example, in an aura that has not been "tuned up" in a while, you may find a number of small lumps or bumps. These can form when you choose to hold onto energy that doesn't belong to you. Although this energy may impact all the layers of the aura, the effect is slight and can be easily cleared with an aura healing.

Whacks, dents, and holes, on the other hand, are more serious than lumps and bumps. As the words imply, these issues of the aura are caused when negative energy is thrown at you, leaving a void, fissure or even opening in your personal space. Whacks, dents, and holes are often experienced by a healer as a cool spot in the aura or a location where there is a lack of pressure on their hands. With time, you may even begin to sense where the edges of the whacks, dents, or holes lie or you may begin to perceive the emotional impact they have on your client.

Whacks, dents, and holes can affect one or all of the seven layers of your aura. As the name implies, some whacks or dents may be so deep that a hole is left in the aura that goes clear through to the physical body. When this occurs, you may find that your client is experiencing physical pain in the body where the core of the whack or hole is found.

Once lumps, bumps, whacks, dents and holes are corrected, the aura is able to once again take on its shiny egg-like appearance. The energy within the aura is able to move and flow properly, which means that you or your client's energy is flowing correctly, thus denoting a state of health and wellness.

Advanced Aura Healing

In this next exercise, we will explore a more in-depth technique you can utilize to heal yourself. In the Simple Aura Healing, you used a squeegee to clear energy from your aura in a general way. Now you are going to clear each layer of your aura, in succession. As you perform this healing on yourself, utilize any other tool you feel comfortable with or seem appropriate to use.

When working on your aura, it is important to ensure that each of the seven layers are smoothed out or healed. Starting with the layer closest to your body and working outward, you will now smooth and fill each layer of your aura. If there are whacks, dents or holes in the aura, imagine them being filled in with healing energy. Sending healing energy from the fourth chakra, down your arm channels and out your hands. Visualize this as a golden white light.

Exercise: The Seven Layer Clearing

Close your eyes and take a deep breath.

Say hello to your body.

Let go of your old grounding cord and create a new one in present time.

Go to your Sacred Space. Straighten up this space if required.

From your Sacred Space, notice your aura, the electromagnetic field around your body.

Your aura should extend all the way around you; in front of you, to the sides of you, all the way around your back and around and under your feet.

Feel the edges of the aura.

Notice how your aura feels to you at this time.

Become aware of how big it is.

Pretend you can pull your aura in until it is 12-18 inches away from your body.

If there is any resistance to bringing your aura in, give yourself permission to release it down your grounding cord.

Take a moment to increase your grounding cord so that it includes your entire aura.

Let your whole space be grounded.

Let anything you want to release in your aura drop down your grounding cord.

Now, holding up one of your hands, pretend that you are holding a squeegee, an ice scraper or any other psychic tool you choose.

Put your hand out and into the first layer of your aura. The first layer of
your aura is the layer that is closest to your body.

Starting at the top of your head, and going down to where your aura
connects with your grounding cord, use your squeegee to clear
the first layer of your aura.

Notice if you feel any lumps, bumps, dents or holes in your aura as you
work.

This is where your energy is stuck in the first layer of your aura.

Say hello to that energy and watch it as it goes down your grounding
cord.

Don't forget to clear your aura behind your back.

Notice how it feels to have this layer cleared of stagnant energy.

Continue this process by moving on to the second layer of your aura,
allowing all the built up energy to be released down your grounding cord.

Notice how it feels to have this layer cleared.

Continue working your way through each layer of your aura, taking a
moment to notice what it feels like to have that layer cleared.

When you are done, take a moment to give to yourself by calling back
your energy from wherever you left it into a sphere of golden
white light above your head.

As you performed this healing on yourself, what pictures or issues
came to mind? Take a moment now to call back your energy from
those situations.

Watch as this energy streams back to you, filling your sphere with
more and more your energy.

Notice how it gets bigger and bigger as you call more and more of
your energy back.

When your sphere is filled, bring that ball of light down and around
your body, clearing your aura, your body and your grounding
cord.

Open your eyes when your body feels full, vital and refreshed. Stretch
out your body, opening your eyes when you feel comfortable.
Were you able to feel each layer of your aura?

Did you notice a difference in the kinds of energy in each layer?

Did you find any lumps, bumps, whacks, or dents in your aura?

What else did you notice as you performed this healing?

Exercise: Using The Seven Layer Clearing On Others

Let's take what you just learned in the previous exercise and put it to work by practicing on someone else. As you do this exercise, be aware of any lumps, bumps, whacks, dents or holes you may find in the aura, filling them in with the golden white light of your healing energy.

Before you begin, prepare yourself first.

To begin, first ground and center your body.

Bring your aura in and around the body and tuck it into your grounding cord.

Set your aura and grounding on release.

Go to your Sacred Space.

Allow your earth, universal and healing energy to start flowing.

You are now ready to begin.

Ask your client "Would you like a healing?".

Once accepted, create a new grounding cord for your client that goes from her first chakra down to the center of the planet, firmly anchoring it into planet and set it on release.

Bring her aura about 12-18 inches away from her body

Tuck her grounding cord into her aura and set it on release.

Using your hands or any psychic tool that feels appropriate, locate the first layer of her aura.

Start at the top of her head; work your way down and around the body, clearing the first layer of her aura.

What did you notice as you cleared this layer of the aura?

Next, locate the second layer of her aura.

Work your way down and around the body clearing the second layer of her aura.

What did you notice as you cleared this layer?

Continue to work your way through each successive layer of her aura, clearing each layer all the way around her body.

After completing the seventh layer, smooth out the entire aura.

Call her energy back into a sphere of golden white light above her head and bring in down and around her body filling her body with her own energy.

Were you able to feel each layer of your client's aura?

Did you notice a difference in the energy of each layer?

Did you find any lumps, bumps, whacks, or dents in your client's aura?

What else did you notice as you performed this healing?

Now take a moment to validate what you have just done. Ask your client: How do you feel now? Do you feel clearer, more present or relaxed?

Did you notice a difference as I worked on one-layer verses another layer?

What else did you notice as I cleared your aura?

Exercise: Fun With Aura Clearing

Here is a fun exercise you can play with as you practice performing aura clearings. I sometimes call this exercise, "Layer, Layer, What's the Layer?" This exercise can be done once you have finished performing an aura clearing. Ask yourself, "Where is the third layer". Allow your hand(s) to guide you into your or your client's aura until they find the third layer. Try locating other layers using this technique.

Another version is when you try to discover what layer your hand(s) have located. Try moving your hand(s) into your client's aura and ask yourself, "What layer is this?"

Trust the information you are receiving. Validate yourself for receiving this information.

Quick Space Clearing

Here is a simple healing technique you can use to give yourself a quick tune up. Notice how quickly you can perform this technique on yourself.

To begin, say hello to your body.
Drop your old grounding cord and create a new one in present time.
Bring your aura in and around your body.
Go to your Sacred Space.
Say hello to your earth, universal and healing energy and allow them to
*   start flowing through your body.*
On your reading screen, create a Q-tip cotton swab.
Take the cotton swab, and starting at the top of your head, imagine that

you can quickly clean out your aura by swirling the cotton swab through it, allowing it to collect any stagnant energy.

Adjust the size of the cotton swab to a size that feels comfortable and appropriate.

Watch as the cotton swab cleans your aura.

If the cotton swab gets too full, drop it down your grounding cord.

When you are done clearing your aura, create another cotton swab and use it to clean out your body, cleaning your head and neck, your torso, your arms and your legs.

Notice how good this feels to your body.

If this cotton swab gets full, drop it down your grounding cord and create a new one to finish this process.

Next, create two cotton swabs and have them run through and clear your leg channels.

Check to see that your earth energy is still flowing.

Drop those cotton swabs down your grounding cord.

Next, create more two cotton swabs and have them clear your back channels, checking that your universal energy is still flowing.

Drop those cotton swabs down your grounding cord.

Finally, create two additional cotton swabs and have them clean out your arm channels, checking that your healing energy is also still flowing.

Also drop those cotton swabs down your grounding cord.

Notice how quickly you were able to clear your space.

Notice how much better your body feels.

Now call back all your energy into a golden white sphere above your head.

Bring that energy down, filling up your aura, your body, and your energy channels.

Take a deep breath, opening your eyes when your body feels full, vital and refreshed.

How did it feel utilizing this technique? Do you feel clearer, lighter, and more present?

Cords

Cords are lines of energy that go from one place to another. For example, a grounding cord is a line of energy that goes from your first chakra to the center of the planet. Cords can also go from one person to another. It is through cords that we communicate with each other non-verbally.

Cords typically are found running from one person's chakra to a chakra in another person. Infants or small children, for example, usually have a cord that runs from their second chakra (their desire or need center) to the mother's first chakra (her survival center). When the child is hungry or needs attention in the middle of the night, s/he sends a communication through the cord to the mother and says, "feed me" or "I need to be changed". It is through this line of energy that a mother will awaken from a dead sleep.

People who are close to each other also have communication cords that run between them. Have you ever had a close friend where you constantly finish each other's sentences? Do you find yourself thinking and your friend utters the same words out loud? Since cords typically go from chakra to chakra there might have been a cord that went from your fifth chakra (your communication center) to your friend's fifth chakra (their communication center), as exemplified in the previous example,

Not all cords, however, are good, positive or beneficial to us. We can also get corded by individuals where there is not a positive communication being interacted. How many times have you experienced the feeling of having a "knife in your back"? This feeling is a cord that happens to be in your back.

As you learn to work with and identify cords, you might find it interesting to look at where the cord is located and what chakra the cord is plugged into. When cords are attached to us in the front of the body, we are usually aware of their presence. We have this person on our conscious mind, or we know it is them calling when the phone rings. We can also have cords that are connected to us on the back of the chakra. We are usually not aware of these cords. Since they are behind us, they are out of our "line of sight" and out of our awareness. Many times people who cord us in the back are afraid of being seen.

Removing undesirable cords is simple to do. When you do find a cord in someone's space, simply grab hold of it and gently and lovingly pull it out. Cords do not respond well to anger, frustration or effort. They will typically go into resistance and want to stay in place. After you have finished pulling out a cord, make sure you seal the hole the cord left in his or her body and aura with a golden white light filled with healing.

Your Healing Master

Your healing master is a spirit guide who has agreed to work with you in this lifetime. While we have many spirit guides, our healing master's primary responsibility is to work with us on **healing** levels.

I have two healing masters who I am working with in this lifetime. They are both very interesting characters. Joe, for example, is a really sweet guy. The valance, or image, he shows me, is that he was in his early twenties during the late 50s, early 60s. He usually wears blue jeans, a white tee shirt and a brown leather jacket. On the outside he appears to be hardened, but he is sensitive and emotional. Lou, on the other hand, is a tough guy. The image he shows me is that he lived in Chicago during the Prohibition. He was a Mafia gangster and appears wearing a pinstriped suit and spats. He's great if I need something specific done or if I'm in a hurry. He's a "get things done" kind of a guy.

Your healing master can take on the appearance of being male or female. They will typically show you the image of their last incarnation here on earth. They can be young or old, tall or short. There is no preset requirement.

We draw our healing master to us based on our own personality. For me, I am direct and specific, thus my healing masters reflection this quality. We think and operate alike. Let's say for example you are like me, in that you are a straightforward individual. What would your relationship with your healing master be if they were emotional or easy going? In turn, if you are an emotional, nurturing individual, how would you feel to have a healing master who was direct or aggressive? We draw our healing masters to us based on our needs and requirements.

Your healing master has incarnated on Earth at some point time. They understand what it is like to live in our world. Like all of us, they have personalities of their own, their own strengths and weakness. I think you will enjoy getting to know your healing master, just as I did.

So let's take a moment and meet your healing master. As you do this exercise, now more than ever, you must trust the information you are receiving. While it may seem or feel as if you are only using your imagination, trust that you are not.

Exercise: Meeting Your Healing Master

Shift your body into a comfortable position and close your eyes.

Let go of all your concerns. Nothing else has to be important during this time. Just let it all go, knowing that you can have it all back later in any way you wish . . .

Now take a long slow deep breath. Hold it in for just a second . . . and then exhale slowly and easily.

Feel your whole body go into a state of rest.

Imagine yourself standing now, at the top of a hill in a picturesque natural setting. Feel your feet on the ground, your head and shoulder easily balanced and relaxed as you look around at the lush trees and greenery.

As you stand on the top of this hill, you notice ahead of you a grove of trees and off to the right and a path going down and into the woods.

Feel the softness of Mother Earth under your feet as you walk down the path. Smell the trees around you. Hear the birds sing . . .

As you walk, you will notice some bends and turns in the path. Follow these going deeper and deeper into the woods . . .

Now ahead of you, through the trees, you see a clearing.

As you come to the clearing, you see a sun-filled meadow dressed in bright and awe inspiring flowers.

Feel the sunshine as it warms your face.

In the distance, you see a small structure. This is the home of your healing master

As you walk closer, you can now see clearly all of the details of the structure including a door with a welcome sign on it. Walk up to this door and turn the knob . . .

Enter the house and look around and notice all the wondrous things that surround you.

Take a deep breath and smell the stimulating aroma.

As you walk further into the house, see before you, sitting in a chair, your healing master.

It stands and walks towards you, welcoming you into its presence. You feel your healing master take your hand. Feel the texture and temperature of your healing master's hand. Notice if it is rough or smooth, young or old. Feel the energy of your healing master's presence filling your awareness . . .

Allow your vision to move from its hand up the arm to the head and shoulders. See your guides face. Look into its eyes. Experience how it regards you. Experience how it is dressed, its sex, and its whole appearance . . .

Feel free to communicate with your healing master. Ask for its name. Ask where it came from or its history. Ask what life lessons you will be working on together. Ask your healing master if there is anything else you should know.

Communicate to your healing master that you would like to work with it on healing levels, assisting you in your healing work.

Ask your healing master to come and stand behind you.

Ask it to place it's hands **in** your hands. Experience how it feels to have your healing master's hands **in** yours.

Now ask it to unplug its hands from yours and have it take a step back out of your space.

Wait a moment or two and then ask your healing master to come and *stand behind you again and place its hands in your hands. Again, experience how this feels.*

Now ask your healing master to unplug from your hands. Have it take a step back and out of your space.

Ask your healing master if you can call upon it again.

Thank your healing master for communicating with you and assure it that you will call upon it again.

Now take a moment to call back some of your energy.

Take a deep breath, opening your eyes when your body feels full, vital and refreshed.

What does your healing master look like?

Was it male or female?

Was it young or old?

Did it tell you its name? What name was given?

What is his/her history?

What lessons is it here to work with you on?

What else did your healing master communicate to you?

Exercise: Aura/Chakra Clearing

In this next exercise, you are going to utilize your healing master to assist you in performing a healing on yourself.

To begin, first close your eyes.

Take a deep breath and come back to your body.

Say hello to your first chakra and connect it to the center of the planet with a new grounding cord.

Bring your energy and attention to your Sacred Space and be there, straightening this space as required.

Allow your earth, universal, and healing energies to begin flowing.

It is through your hands that the healing energy of your healing master will be channeled.

Become aware of your hand chakras in the middle of your palms.

You might feel them tingle or become warm.

From the center of your head, call in your healing master, and ask him or her to connect into the back of hand chakras.

Say hello to your healing master.

Take a deep breath and relax back into your body once again.

Ask your healing master to help you construct a new grounding cord.

Create a mental picture as you instruct him what kind of grounding cord you would like to have.

Allow your body to release any unwanted energy from your body down your grounding cord.

Notice how good it feels to your body to have a new grounding cord.

Take a deep breath.

Have your healing master locate your first chakra and show it to you.

Tell your healing master that this chakra handles your survival energy and information and is also where you have your grounding cord attached.

Look at your first chakra on your reading screen. What do you notice about it?

Have your healing master remove the foreign energy built up around the chakra and repair any damage found there.

Ask your healing master to show you any cords that might be connected to your first chakra and remove them.

Can feel your healing master working there?

Do you notice any changes?

Now take a deep breath and relax into your body once again.

Does it feel any different from when you started this healing?

Next, ask your Healing Master to show you your second chakra.

This is where your ability of clairsentience, your ability to feel energy is centered.

Ask your healing master to clear out any unwanted energy and repair any damage done to it.

Have your healing master remove all of the cords from this chakra.

Ask your healing master to whom the cord(s) belong.

What answer did you receive?

Notice all the changes in your awareness as your healing master works.

Notice your body. How does it feel?

Take a deep breath.

Now direct your healing master to locate and show you your third chakra.

This chakra handles your ability to use your power.

Let your healing master clean out your third chakra and repair it.

Are there any cords going into your third chakra?

Who is tying into your energy?

Have your healing master remove the cords from this chakra.

Are you starting to feel more relaxed, more present?

What changes do you notice now?

Take a deep breath.

Have your healing master show you your fourth chakra, or heart center, which is located in the middle of your chest.

This chakra contains your ability to love yourself unconditionally.

In what condition is your self-love chakra?

Does it have so much of other people's energy and considerations in it that you have a difficult time loving yourself?

Have the healing master take everyone else's needs and desires out of your fourth chakra.

Also have your healing master remove any cords found there.

Notice how much more space you have in your chest area.

Next, let's move onto your fifth chakra.

The fifth chakra is located right by the cleft in your throat.

This chakra deals with your ability to communicate.

Have your healing master repair any damages and removing any cords found there.

Notice what happens to you as your healing master works on your fifth chakra.

Is your head less noisy or stuffy?

What else do you notice as your healing master assists you in cleaning out your fifth chakra?

Breathe deeply and relax into your body once again.

Have your healing master show you your sixth chakra. The sixth chakra or third eye is located just above the eyes in the center of the forehead.

This is where your ability to clairvoyance or clear seeing is centered.

It is in this space that you visualize, that you see the world in your mind's eye.

Have your healing master clear out any old pictures or judgments that keep you from seeing clearly; clearing out anyone else's pictures or judgments that also may be in this space.

Ask your healing master to remove any cords found here also.

Take a deep breath.

Let's move on to the seventh chakra.

The seventh chakra, the chakra of knowingness, is located on the top of your head.

It contains your ability to just know information without it being pro-cessed by the rest of the body or chakras. This is also the place where we receive information from our God, our Higher Self, the Supreme Being or whatever name you choose to use.

Have your healing master show you this chakra.

What do you notice about it?

Ask your healing master to remove any foreign energy built up around it and removing any cords found.

Take a deep breath.

Notice how it good feels to have more of your own body, your space for yourself.

Notice how it feels to have your chakras cleared of unwanted energy.

Ask your healing master to unplug from the backs of your hands and take a step back, moving out of your space.

Ask your healing master to create a ball of golden white light above your head, filling it with the energy of your highest good, healing and your amusement.

Have your healing master bring that ball of your energy down and around your body, bringing some of it in through your seventh chakra.

Allow it to wash through your body, flowing through each chakra down to the first chakra, restoring and revitalizing each one.

When your chakras are filled, allow this energy to radiate from the chakras out through the rest of your body.

Notice how it feels to be filled with your own life force energy.

Thank your healing master for assisting you in this healing.

Now ask him/her to return to where he/she came from.

When your body feels full, vital and refreshed, stretch out your body, opening your eyes when you feel comfortable.

Could you feel your healing master assisting you with this healing? What else did you notice as you worked with your healing master?

Did you find stagnant energy on and around your chakras? Was it concentrated on one chakra verses another. If so, which chakras?

Did you find many cords plugged into your chakras? Were there more cords going into one chakra verses another. If so, which chakras?

How do you feel now that you have healed yourself? Clearer, balanced, more grounded?

What did you notice as you gave yourself this healing?

Exercise: Aura/Chakra Clearing In Others

In performing an aura/chakra clearing, we take the basic concepts of aura clearing or aura fluffing one step further by working on energies within the aura, the chakras and energy channels in others. In this exercise, we will also be calling upon the guidance and assistance or our healing masters.

To begin, ground and center your body.

Check to see that your aura is tucked around your body and firmly connected to your grounding cord.

Set your grounding cord on release.

Go to your Sacred Space.

Allow your earth, universal and healing energy to start flowing.

Ask your healing master to come and stand behind you, plugging her hands into yours.

You are now ready to begin the healing.

Start by asking your client "Would you like a healing?".

Create a new grounding cord for your client and set it on release.

Bring her aura in until it is about 12-18 inches away from her body.

Tuck her aura into her grounding cord and set it on release.

Check and smooth out her aura as required.

Starting at your client's feet, ask your healing master to assist you in clearing your client's feet chakra.

Using any tools that seem appropriate, scoop, dust or smooth unwanted energy from her feet chakra.

Ask your healing master to assist your in bringing clean, fresh energy up from Mother Earth.

Allow this energy to tickle the bottoms of your client's feet.

Next, ask your healing master to assist you in bringing your client's earth energy in through her feet, up her calves, through her knees and up her thighs, to her first chakra, releasing the energy down her grounding cord.

Using any tools that seem appropriate, scoop, dust or smooth any unwanted energy out your client's first chakra.

Check to see if there are any cords attached to this chakra.

Have your healing master assist you in removing any cords you encounter.

What do you notice as you clean out this space? Ask your healing master what this energy is. Acknowledge the answer you get in return.

Check to ensure that her grounding cord is still going down to the center of the earth and is set on release.

Create a new grounding cord for your client if necessary.

Scoop, dust or smooth any unwanted energy out her grounding cord and out of the connection between the grounding cord and the first chakra.

When you have completed this, move up and clear the second chakra.

Again, scoop, dust or smooth any unwanted energy out her second chakra, asking your healing master what the energy is.

Have your healing master assist you in removing any cords from her second chakra.

Continue to work your way up the body, chakra by chakra, until you reach the seventh chakra.

When you have completed the seventh chakra, have your client take a deep breath.

Take a step behind your clients, so that you are facing her back.

Starting at the top of her head, at the seventh chakra, have your healing master assist you bring clean, clear universal energy down through your client's seventh chakra, down her back channels and into her first chakra.

If you feel any resistance as you bring universal energy into her body, ask your healing master what the resistance is and ask them to assist you in clearing it.

Walk around your client, so that you are facing her front.

Bring a mixture of universal energy and earth energy up their front channels.

Work with your healing master to clear out any blockages or resistance.

Allow this mixture to spout out into your client's aura, filling their aura with their own life force energy.

Have your client take a deep breath.

Next, scoop, dust or smooth any unwanted energy from her hand chakras.

Starting at the fourth chakra, the heart center, have your healing master assist you in cleaning out the energy channels that run from the fourth chakra through the arms and out the hands.

Have your client take a deep breath.

Take a deep breath yourself.

Smooth her aura, repairing any lumps, bumps, dents or whacks you may find.

Create a ball of golden white light above your client's head, calling back all of her energy, filling the ball of light with health, healing and amusement.

Bring the ball of light down and around her body.

Have your client take one last deep breath.

Say to your client, "With each breath you take, allow yourself to release any unwanted energy from every muscle, gland, and organ of your body, right down to the cellular level."

She is being filled and renewed with her own life force energy.

Ask your healing master to unplug from your hands and take a step back.

Thank your healing master for assisting you in the healing.

Tell them to return to whence they came.

Take a step back from your client.

Tell your client she can move around, stretch or get up, whenever she feels comfortable.

After each healing session, record your observations, asking your client what her experiences were receiving the healing.

Client name/Date:

Client name/Date:

Client name/Date:

Client name/Date:

Client name/Date:

Client name/Date:

Client name/Date:

Clairsentient Healing—Wrapping It All Up

Let's take this concept to the next stage. Up until this point, while performing healings, we have been using a process or formula, going from point A to point B in successive steps. This is a great way in which to learn a new tool or technique. But remember, it is just a guideline.

In this exercise, improvise upon the procedure asking your healing master to guide your hands to the *appropriate location* for you to work. Trust that your healing master will guide and direct you in performing the work that needs to be done. Ask your healing master to reveal to you the underlying nature of the energy or issues your client is working on. Trust the feelings or impressions you receive. Communicate these impressions to your client. After each session record your observations and ask your client to share her experience with you.

Client name/Date:

Client name/Date:

Client name/Date:

Working With The Energy Around You

Energetic Protection

As energetic beings, we are constantly being influenced by other people's energy. It is a natural occurrence. It happens to all of us. Our chakras are designed to pick-up and interpret information from the world around us. We bring in and utilize this energetic information much like a cat uses it's whiskers. It helps to guide us in our daily life.

Many times, however, when we pick up or match the energy around us, we make the assumption is that the energy is our own. We carry it around in our aura, clouding our ability to separate our feelings and emotions from those of others. There are, however, ways to protect yourself from picking up this energy in the first place. Let's take a deeper look at the kinds of energy I am speaking about.

When you have interactions with your friends, family or relatives, you are influenced by their energy. For example, think about the time you had a conversation with a friend who just lost a loved one. Did you find yourself going into sympathy with their pain, perhaps becoming upset, hurt or angry? Then think about the time you spoke with a friend just started a new romantic relationship. As you spoke to them did you find that you became excited or giddy. Have you ever noticed that even though you did not feel these emotions prior to the conversation, but in the end, you somehow wound up walking away much as your friend or loved one did? You have just taken on or "matched" their energy.

You can also pick up energy as you walk around the supermarket, the mall, or even the movie theater. Think about how many times have you gone to the mall on Christmas Eve and felt overwhelmed, irritable, tired or anxious? What you were doing was picking up and matching the emotions and energy of the all of the people in the mall.

The easiest way to insulate yourself from unwanted energy is to clearly identify the edges of your aura, the boundaries of your personal space. Earlier, you learned how to expand and contract your aura. This gave you an idea as to the boundaries of your own personal space. Once the boundaries of the aura are identified, you can place an object on the edge of our aura to remind you that this is **your** aura, **your** space, and you don't have to share it with anyone. This will also show other people energetically the edges of your space. Once your boundaries are set, you can choose what energies you would like to process as your own, excluding those you do not want.

In addition, this will assist you in differentiating who you are, what your needs and desires are and the needs and desires of those around you. I would like for you to postulate that you can now recognize when you take on other people's energy. By recognizing that the energy does not belong to you, you are giving yourself permission to let it go.

Exercise: Creating A Protection Mirror

In the following exercise, you will explore ways in which to not be affected by the energy around you.

To begin, first close your eyes, then ground and center your body.
Tuck your aura in around your body.
Set your aura and grounding on release.
Go to your Sacred Space.
Allow your earth, universal and healing energy to start flowing.
Bring your aura about 12-18 inches around your body.

On your reading screen, create a mirror. This mirror can be any size and shape you wish.

Place the mirror on the outside or the seventh layer of your aura, positioned in front of the heart center or fourth chakra.

Make sure the mirror is placed with its reflective surface facing away from your body.

Give your mirror a grounding cord that goes all the way down to the center of the planet.

Imagine your protection mirror reflecting off any unwanted energy.

Notice how it feels to have your protection mirror in place.

Do you feel safer? More protected?

Does your space feel more contained with it in place?

Now, try removing your mirror from your aura.

That's right; just throw it into your "psychic" garbage can.

Now how does your space feel?

Did you notice a shift in your energy when you removed it?

Okay . . . let's place a new protection mirror on the outside of the seventh layer of your aura.

Don't forget to ground your new protection mirror and envision it reflecting off any energy that is inharmonious to your health, well being and highest good.

Like your grounding cord, your protection mirror also needs to be checked regularly, being cleaned or replaced in order to ensure that it is functioning correctly.

Practice creating and removing your protection mirror.

Notice how it feels each time.

What did your protection mirror look like? Was it big, small, square, round?

How did you feel when you have your protection mirror in place?

How did you feel when you remove your protection mirror?

What else did you notice when you had your protection mirror in place?

Exercise: Using Your Protection Mirror

To do this exercise, you will need to enlist the help of a friend or client. You can practice this exercise at work or when interacting with family members.

To begin, have your client sit in a chair across from you.
Ask her to relate to you a problem or issue she is currently experiencing or a sad story she would like to share.
Allow her to convey her story uninterrupted for a minute or two.
Check in with your feelings as she conveys her story to you.
Become aware of what you body feels like as she tells you her story.

How does your energy feel to you now?

Did you empathize with her story? Why or why not?

What else did you notice about the interaction?

Take a short break ... Get up and walk around for a few minutes. Then return to your chair and try this exercise again, except this time, use your protection mirror.
Take a deep breath.
Close your eyes.
Ground and center your body here in present time.

Bring your aura is in and around your body.
Set your grounding and aura on release.
Go to your Sacred Space.
Allow your earth, universal and healing energy to start flowing.
Create a protection mirror.
Place your protection mirror on the seventh layer of your aura in front
*   of your fourth chakra.*
Give your protection mirror a grounding cord.
Have your mirror reflect off any unwanted energy.
Once prepared, ask your client to relate to you the same problem or
*   issue.*
Allow her to convey her story uninterrupted for a minute or two.
As she talks, check in with what you are feeling.

Did you notice a difference when she relayed her story to you? What was it?

Was it easier to listen to her problem?

Did you go into empathy or sympathize with her?

Did you notice a separation between your emotions and hers?

What else did you notice about the interaction?

Ask your client if they noticed a difference between the first time she related her story verses the second time. Record her response.

Protecting Your Work Environment

Your aura is the personal space around your body. It is your personal bubble. It acts as a layer of protection from the world around you. Like your body, it is a good idea to also say hello to the aura of the room where you do your work, thus making it a safer place for you to be.

A room like your aura, grounding cord and even reading screen can and do have the energy in and around them stagnate and now flow freely. By working with the energy in a room, you can reduce the amount of resistance or energy in your environment, thus facilitating your psychic work and healings. This is especially helpful when working with clients.

The following exercise is a simple technique to use and master. It can be used wherever you are, such as at home, at work and even in other meeting spaces such as when you meet with your doctor or lawyer. I think you will be surprised at the results you experience.

Exercise: Working With The Energy In A Room

To begin, take a deep breath.

Close your eyes.

Ground and center your body here in present time.

Check to see if your aura is in around your body and firmly connected to your grounding cord.

Set your grounding and aura on release.

Go to your Sacred Space.

Allow your earth, universal and healing energy to start flowing.

Create a brand new protection mirror and place it on the seventh layer of your aura.

Don't forget to ground it.

Grounding a room is a simple thing to do.

Think of the walls of the room as being the edges of an enormous balloon, or the boundaries of a giant aura.

Create an oversized grounding cord in the center of the room that goes all the way down to the center of the planet.

In your mind's eye, tuck the giant aura (the walls) into the grounding cord.

That's right, just like you have learned to do with your body.

Set the room's aura on release.

Watch as the energy drains out of the space.

Notice how this feels to your body.

As yourself "If the room were vibrating at a particular color, what color would that be?"

How does this color make you feel?

You can change the color in a room as easily as you can change the color of the energy running through your energy channels.

Change the color in the room to one that feels good to your body.

What color did you change it to?

Could you feel the energy shift around you?

What else do you notice as you change the color of the room's vibration?

Now, place a protection mirror on the outside of your room's aura.

Place the mirror where it feels appropriate

This will protect your workspace from unwanted energy just like when you put a protection mirror on your aura.

How does this feel to your body?

If you want, try giving your room a healing, performing the same technique you used on yourself to heal your aura, except on a much larger scale.

What do you notice as you do this?

When you are done, working on the room, take a moment to call back some of your energy, stretching your body and opening your eyes when you are done

What did you notice after you grounded the aura of the room?

What did you notice when you changed the color in which your space was vibrating?

What else did you notice as you worked with the aura of your workspace?

Exercise: Creating A Safe Work Space

When you work with a client, you can also create an aura around yourself and your client, which I call a reading aura. A reading aura, just like your personal aura is a wall of energy that can protect you and your client from energy in the room or space around you. I have found that a reading aura can reduce distractions experienced while working with your psychic information. This is especially helpful if working in a room with other people.

First, prepare yourself to work with your client by creating a new grounding cord, bringing your aura in and around your body, getting your energy flowing and bringing your energy and attention to your Sacred Space.

Create a protection mirror on the outside of your aura and ground it.

Say hello to the room you are working in, making it a safe space in which to be.

Next, create a reading aura around yourself and your client.

This sphere can look any way you want. It can appear as a soap bubble or as a colored glass ball, a balloon or as if it were made of crystal.

Ask your healing master what is should look like.

What answer did you get?

Like your own aura, give your reading aura a grounding cord and set it on release.

Put a protection mirror on the outside of this space.

Test your new reading aura by performing a reading or healing.

What did you notice as you performed the reading or healing? Did you have more concentration?

Were you able to focus easier?

Dissipating Energy

By now, you should now be familiar with how your energy works within your body. You may find times, however, where your energy slows down or gets stuck. This can occur when you are working on a project or you are processing information. It can feel as if you have a weight on your shoulders, a heaviness in your hearts, or confusion in your life.

Sometimes when you try to release the stagnant energy from your space, instead of just letting it go, you choose to go into effort or resistance. This can be true even after you have given yourself a healing. You may discover that you are still holding on to a situation or issue. There may also be times when you are a working with a client and find yourself matching her energy.

Dissipating energy is an easy way to quickly move unwanted energy out of your space at any time. Like calling your energy back to yourself, you can dissipate energy whether you are grounded or not, on the phone or in the tub. If you feel that there is stagnant energy in your space, simply imagine that you are moving this energy out of your body and aura.

You can do this by imagining you are filling an empty sphere with stagnant energy. Then as quickly and as easily as you created it, you can move the sphere away from your body, imaging a piece of dynamite under it and blowing it up. By blowing up the energy, you are allowing it to be dissipated. This image also gives you the opportunity to bring in a little of your amusement. The dissipated energy is then transformed into neutral energy. You can create as many new spheres as you need to pull all the stagnant energy from your space.

You can also use this tool to let go of a specific energy or emotion. This can be accomplished by allowing all of the energy of a specific person, place, issue, or situation to flow into the sphere. We will explore this concept in the next exercise.

Exercise: Dissipating Energy From Your Space

Let's try utilizing this tool in the form of a meditation.

Close your eyes and say hello to your body.

Create a new grounding cord, bring your aura in and around your body and set both on release.

Get your earth, universal and healing energy flowing.

Create a protection mirror and place it on the seventh layer of your aura.

Create a clear sphere out in front of you.

Now, allow all of the energy, that doesn't belong to you, or energy that you want to move out of your aura, your body and your space and go into the sphere.

Have the unwanted energy appear as little black dots.

Watch as they fly from your space and fill up the sphere.

When it is all filled up, move the sphere out of your space.

With amusement, watch as the energy in the sphere quickly dissipates, as if you had placed a stick of dynamite underneath the sphere.

Watch as it explodes dissipating all of that energy that did not belong to you.

How does it feel to have unwanted energy moved out of your space?

Keep creating energy spheres and dissipating unwanted energy until if feels complete.

Fill in all the places you just released energy by summoning back your own healing energy.

How did it feel as you removed unwanted energy from your space?

What did you notice after you had dissipated this energy?

What else did you notice as you dissipated unwanted energy from your space?

Exercise: Dissipating Specific Energies

Let's try a moving a few specific energies out of your space. Record your results as you go.
Fear:

Effort:

Anger:

Frustration:

Jealousy:

A friend or family member:

Exercise: Dissipating Energy In Others

Similar to dissipating our own energy, we can also move energy that has stagnated in our client's space into a sphere in front of them. This is a wonderful technique for you to use if your client is resistant to letting go of a specific energy in their space.

By utilizing this technique, you can move the energy from their body and aura, but leave it close enough to them to look at it or bring it back into their space if desired. This will allow your client to experience what it feels like to have their personal space free of this energy. This will give them the opportunity to decide it they want to let the trapped energy go or not.

Prepare yourself first.

Create a new grounding cord and set it on release.
Bring your aura in and around your body, setting it on release.
Get your earth, universal and healing energies flowing.
Place a new protection mirror on the outside of your aura.
You are now ready to begin the healing.
Ask your client if there is a specific problem, project or issue she is working on.
Say hello to the project or issue in your client's body and aura.
Collect the energy into a sphere in front of her.
Are you noticing any resistance as you try to move this energy?
Reassure your client that she can hold onto the energy if she chooses; that you are only moving the energy outside of her space, placing it in a location where she can see it whenever she wants.
Tell her that she can let it go or have it back any time if she chooses.
Now, collect the energy into the sphere.
Was it easier this time?
Move the sphere of energy out of her aura and place it to her side, just above her line of sight.
Show her where you put the sphere containing her project or issue.
Give the sphere a grounding cord and set on release.
Call back her energy and fill her body and aura with a golden white light, filling the void where her project or issue was once located.

What did you notice as you moved the project or issue into a sphere and out of your client's space?

Did you experience less resistance once you reassured your client that she could have her energy back if she chose to?

Now ask your client the following questions:
How does she feel now that you have moved the project or issue out of her space? Does she feel lighter, less weighed down?

What else did she notice as you performed this healing?

Working With Energy On Clairvoyant Levels

Clairvoyance

When you look at things clairvoyantly, you are viewing things through your mind's eyes, on our *reading* screen utilizing an inherent ability of the sixth chakra. It refers not only to your ability to see mental image pictures, but as you will discover, it is your ability to look at energy. It is from this clairvoyant space that you will also learn how to work with or manipulate the energy that you see, as well as communicate what you are looking at.

You have been using your clairvoyant abilities throughout this book, when you created and looked at your reading screen, your grounding cord and your Sacred Space. You were also using your clairvoyant abilities when you saw your healing master. In this next section you will be utilizing this ability to **look** at specific energies within the body as well as exploring some tools that will allow you to access the answers to questions and issues.

Up until this point in time, as you worked with energy, you noticed and observed energy. In this next section, you will not only notice and observe energy; you will now begin to communicate back to your client what you are looking at. This is a big step when working with clients. Instead of asking your client for validation, you will be receiving validation from your client throughout the session. This can be through a look of recognition in their eyes, a nod of the head or even the look of astonishment.

The key to working with and validating your clairvoyant abilities is to not be afraid to communicate what you are looking at to your client. Be in your integrity. What you see is what you see. If you walk in your truth, then you will only see truth.

How To Begin A Clairvoyant Reading Or Healing

As we have been doing all along, it is important to prepare yourself prior to performing any kind of work on energetic levels, including clairvoyant readings and healing. This ensures that your space is clear and your energy is flowing. Let's review everything we have covered so far and put it into one procedure for preparing yourself for doing work on clairvoyant levels. With practice, it should only take a few seconds to go through.

Exercise: A Preparation Summary

First take a deep breath and say hello to your body.

Clean off your reading screen with a feather duster or Windex window cleaner.

Drop any old grounding cords you may have and create a new one in present time.

Bring your aura twelve to eighteen inches from your body, tucking it into your grounding cord.

Set your aura and grounding on release.

Bring your energy and attention up to your sixth chakra and go to your Sacred Space.

Clean out your Sacred Space as required.

Bring clean and fresh energy up from Mother Earth up through the feet, calves, knees and thighs and into the first chakra, opening or closing your feet chakra to a size comfortable for you.

Allow your earth energy to be released down your grounding cord.

Take a deep breath and enjoy the feeling of having your earth energy running.

Open up the seventh chakra and call in your universal energy.

Bring it down to your seventh chakra and have it flow through your back channels starting at the top of your head, running along either side of the spine, and continuing down to the first chakra.

Using a mixture of universal energy and earth energy, bring this mixture up the front channels, having it fountain out your seventh chakra and filling your aura.

Branch off about 30% of this mixture at the fourth chakra, the heart center, and have your healing energy flow up to the shoulders, through the arms and out your hand chakras.

Open or close your seventh chakra to a size comfortable for you.

Clear your aura, chakras and energy channels as required.

Take a deep breath and relax back into your body.

Let your body feel good with this.

Call back your energy into a ball of golden white light.

As you bring this energy into your aura, your body and your energy channels, give yourself permission to release any energy that has stagnated there.

Ground the room you are in, tucking the room's aura into it's grounding cord and setting it on release.

Create a sphere out in front of you and dissipate unwanted energy from your space as required.

Take a deep breath and call back more of your energy.

If working with a client:

Create a reading space aura and ground that space.

Again, using a sphere, dissipate any energy as required.

At the beginning of clairvoyant reading or healing session you should always ask your client to say their full name for you a few times.

Quickly, check your aura, your grounding and your protection mirror again to ensure they are still working.

Dissipate any energy as required.

Begin the session.

Using Gauges For Yourself

Gauges are tools each of us can use to measure energy. Gauges are great for answering specific questions. They can be employed to answer simple Yes or No questions, measure how open or closed a chakra is, how much we are in agreement to something, or how far in a cycle or process we have come.

Gauges can take on many forms. Yes/No gauges can look like a stop light, with the green meaning yes and the red meaning no. They can even look like a signboard similar to those you find at a baseball or football game, with the words being written out YES!!! Or NO!!! Percent gauges can look like a car's speedometer or a thermometer. They can even have a digital readout. I use different types of gauges for different applications.

For example, when I need the answer to a yes or no question, I will use a signboard with the words Yes or No appearing with my answer. When I am looking at how open or closed a chakra is, I use a digital readout gauge. I find that it is the quickest and easiest to read. On the other hand, when I am looking at how far someone has gone in a process or how much in agreement they are to an idea, I always use a gauge that has a scale of 1 to 100 so that I can view concepts in terms of percentages.

Exercise: Creating A Gauge

Gauges are a simple psychic tools to master. To use a gauge, first identify which type of gauge you would like to use and visualize this gauge on your reading screen. For this example, let's start by using a gauge that looks like a signboard, with yes or no appearing in big bold letters on the board. To use this gauge, ask yourself:

Am I in agreement with using this gauge?

Now let's try this again. Create a new gauge in your mind's eye. This time, however, let's try adding a grounding cord to the bottom of the gauge. Allow the gauge to drain off any excess or stagnant energy down to the center of the planet. This energy can keep you from utilizing the gauge properly. When you are done, again ask yourself:

Am I in agreement with using this gauge?

Did you notice a difference between the first and the second time you asked for an answer? This is because energy such as fear or insecurities can get in the way of your information. By grounding your gauge, you are releasing the energies that get in between you and your information. It is important to create a new gauge for each question you ask and to ground your gauge each time you use one.

Exercise: Gauges And Chakras

In this next exercise, you will be looking at how much of your own energy you are utilizing in each of your chakras. When looking at the chakras, I like using a gauge that appears as a digital readout, like those seen on a watch or clock. Try using this gauge and see how it works for you. When you are done, feel free to try this exercise utilizing a different kind of gauge. Try doing this exercise daily, until you feel comfortable with it.

To begin, first prepare yourself for doing a clairvoyant reading. Then, starting at your first chakra, ask yourself the following questions, answering each question in the form of a percentage.

"How much am I utilizing the energy of my first chakra?"
"How much am I utilizing the energy of my second chakra?"
"How much am I utilizing the energy of my third chakra?"
"How much am I utilizing the energy of my fourth chakra?"
"How much am I utilizing the energy of my fifth chakra?"
"How much am I utilizing the energy of my sixth chakra?"

"How much am I utilizing the energy of my seventh chakra?"

There are no right or wrong answers when looking at chakras. They are where they need to be at any given moment. Remember, they are processing information from the world around us, opening and closing as required. You might find it interesting to repeat this exercise on yourself a few times though out the course of a day, or a few days a week or even both. As you do this, look to see if there are any patterns with regard to your energy, meaning do certain chakras remain a certain percent open while others fluctuate? What does this tell you about your energy?

Exercise: Percent Or Process Gauges

Gauges can also be used to answer questions such as how much you are in agreement with something or how far in a process or cycle you have come. For these types of questions, I always use a percent gauge, with a scale that goes from 1 to 100.

Here are a few questions you can ask yourself. At the end of this exercise, make up a few of your own questions. Ask your higher self for the answers. As you ask yourself these questions, note what thoughts, ideas or concepts come to mind. They can be invaluable clues to your true, underlying feelings.

Remember to create a new gauge for each question you ask yourself. If you are experience a problem answering these questions, check to ensure that you are grounded and that your energy is still flowing. In addition, try to dissipate any energy surrounding the problem or issue you are encountering.

To begin, first prepare yourself to do a clairvoyant reading. As you ask yourself the following questions, record any additional impressions you receive surrounding the initial question. When you are ready, ask yourself the following questions, answering each question in the form of a percentage.

What percent do I like my current job?

What percent do I like where I currently live?

What percent am I enjoying my current relationship with _____?

What percent do I love myself?

How far am I toward loving myself unconditionally?

Now try asking your own questions.
Question/Percentage:

Question/Percentage:

Question/Percentage:

Question/Percentage:

Question/Percentage:

Using Gauges To Look At Others

Once you feel comfortable with utilizing gauges to perform readings on yourself, you will be able to explore how to use this tool to perform a reading on someone else. Trust the information you are receiving while doing this exercise and communicate your findings to your client without judgment. As you communicate each answer, take a moment to see if there is any additional information or clarifications that need to be said. Allow your client to validate your findings. I think you will be surprised at how accurate you will be.

Exercise: A Simple Chakra Reading

In this first exercise, you will look at how open or closed other people chakras are.

First prepare for the reading.
Have your client sit in a chair directly across from you with her feet flat on the floor.
Ask her to keep her eyes open.
Next, prepare yourself for the reading.
When you are ready, create a gauge in your mind's eye and grounding it.
Starting at your client's first chakra, ask yourself:

How much is she utilizing the energy of her first chakra?

How much is she utilizing the energy of her second chakra?

How much is she utilizing the energy of her third chakra?

How much is she utilizing the energy of her fourth chakra?

How much is she utilizing the energy of her fifth chakra?

How much is she utilizing the energy of her sixth chakra?

How much is she utilizing the energy of her seventh chakra?

Practice this exercise as often as possible and on as many different clients as possible.

Exercise: A Simple Percent Or Process Reading

In this exercise, you will be looking at how much in agreement or how far in a process or cycle your client is. Listed below are a few questions to help you get started. As you become comfortable with this exercise, you can disregard the questions listed, allowing your client to ask you questions directly.

Please note that percent readings can be a bit more tricky than performing chakra readings. Many times a client will ask a question such as, "Will I stay in this relationship?" or "Should I stay at my job?" It is up to you to convert your client's questions into a format that is compatible with this exercise. For example, the question," Will I stay in this relationship?" should instead be phrased as "How much in agreement is _____ (client's name) in staying in her current relationship?" In the same way, the question, "Should I stay at my job?" would be rephrased to a question such as "How much in agreement is _____ (client's name) with her job?" Once you convert your client's question, it is easy to provide you client with an answer.

Have your client ask you the questions listed below or a question of her own. As she asks you a question, notice what additional thoughts, ideas or concepts come to mind. They can be invaluable clues to your client's underlying feelings. Communicate these impressions to your client.

First prepare for the reading.

Have your client sit in a chair directly across from you with her feet flat on the floor.

Ask her to keep her eyes open.

Next, prepare yourself for the reading.

When you are ready, create a gauge in your mind's eye and grounding it.

When you are ready, ask yourself:

What percent does she like her jobs?

What percent do she like where she is currently live?

What percent does she enjoy her relationship with _____?

What percent do she love herself?

How far is she toward loving herself unconditionally?

Now allow your client to ask you a few questions. If you feel that clarification of any point is important, communicate this to your client. Be aware of your client's responses to your answers. Were you being validated? As you complete this exercise, ask your client for feedback on the session.

Question/Percentage:

Question/Percentage:

Question/Percentage:

Question/Percentage:

Question/Percentage:

Exercise: A Simple Energy Check

Energy checks are a fun and simple way to combine all of the skills you have learned so far. Energy checks are an excellent way to look at where someone's energy is at any given moment and also a wonderful format to use while performing healing work on clairvoyant levels. While this exercise is formatted to work with a client, it is also a great tool you can use to look at your own energy. To do an energy check, follow the simple instruction below and have fun!

If you need any additional forms to practice on, there is a blank form in Appendix A, which you can use to make copies.

To begin, first prepare yourself for doing a reading.
Ask your client if she would like an energy check.
On your reading screen, ask yourself at the following:

Grounding
What does her grounding cord look like?

How long is it? (Does it go all the way to the center of the planet?)

Is her grounding cord releasing energy? (Yes/No)

Is her grounding cord in present time? (Yes/No)

The Aura

Where is her aura in relationship to her body?

Does it go all the way around the body, including around her feet? (Yes/No)

Does her aura tuck into her grounding cord? (Yes/No)

Is her aura set on release? (Yes/No)

Chakras

Starting at your client's first chakra, create a gauge and ask yourself:

How much is she utilizing the energy of her first chakra?

How much is she utilizing the energy of her second chakra?

How much is she utilizing the energy of her third chakra?

How much is she utilizing the energy of her fourth chakra?

How much is she utilizing the energy of her fifth chakra?

How much is she utilizing the energy of her sixth chakra?

How much is she utilizing the energy of her seventh chakra?

Questions
Question/Percentage:

Question/Percentage:

Question/Percentage:

Question/Percentage:

Question/Percentage:

Healing On Clairvoyant Levels

In this section, we will explore how to look at and work with energy on even deeper levels of healing. In the Aura/Chakra, clearings you utilized your clairsentience to locate stagnant energy in the aura and chakras through touch. When working with gauges and in the Simple Energy Check, you began using your clairvoyant abilities to look at energy. In this next section, you will be delving even further into looking at energy, working and stretching your ability to see and work with energy clairvoyantly.

Exercise: The Gingerbread Man

I find it easier to work on myself if I utilize my reading screen to perform a healing, in that I can not only feel the energy, I see it as well. In addition to working with my reading screen while performing deeper levels of self-healing, I may also visualize myself using the image of a "gingerbread man".

Sometimes, it is difficult to look at ourselves, especially if our energy is stagnant or blocked, or if our aura or chakras are misshapen. By utilizing an image like a gingerbread man, other than creating amusement in my own space, it also helps me to remain neutral to whatever energy I may find.

To do this exercise, first prepare yourself for a reading. Then visualize yourself, or your client, in the form of a gingerbread man on your reading screen.

To begin, first prepare yourself for performing a reading, asking yourself: What does your gingerbread man look? Does it have two arms and legs, a head? Describe its physical appearance.

Grounding
Look at the gingerbread man's grounding cord on your reading screen. Does the gingerbread man have a grounding cord? (Yes/No)

What does it look like?

Does it go all the way down to the center of the planet? (Yes/No)

Create a new grounding cord in present time.
Next, pretend that you have a handful of magic purple dust. Toss the

dust at your grounding cord with the intent that the magic purple dust will turn black and stick to any stagnant energy it finds in your grounding cord.

What do you notice as you do this?

Using a feather duster, your hand, your trusty squeegee or whatever tool feels right, clean off all the black dots from your grounding cord.

Was there stagnant energy in your grounding cord? (Yes/No)

Where was it located?

The Aura

Look at the aura of the Gingerbread man on your reading screen.

What does it look like?

Does it go all the way around its body? (Yes/No)

Bring your aura down and around the gingerbread man's body, tucking it into its grounding cord.

Toss the magic purple dust on its aura, with the intention that it will stick and turn black wherever it finds stagnate energy.

Clean off all the black dots you find in its aura.

Did you find much stagnant energy in its aura? (Yes/No)

Was it in one area of the aura versus another? Please explain.

The Chakras

Look at your first chakra on your reading screen.

What does your first chakra look like?

Toss the magic purple dust on its aura, with the intention that it will stick and turn black wherever it finds stagnate energy.
Clean off all of the black dots from your first chakra.
Did you find much stagnant energy on the chakra? (Yes/No)

Using your reading screen, look at each of the six remaining major chakras, as well as on your hand and feet chakras.
Using the magic purple dust, continue cleaning any stagnant energy you find. Record your observations.
What did your second chakra look like? Was there much stagnant energy on the chakra?

What did your third chakra look like? Was there much stagnant energy on the chakra?

What did your fourth chakra look like? Was there much stagnant energy on the chakra?

What did your fifth chakra look like? Was there much stagnant energy on the chakra?

What did your sixth chakra look like? Was there much stagnant energy on the chakra?

What did your seventh chakra look like? Was there much stagnant energy on the chakra?

What did your hand chakras look like? Was there much stagnant energy on the chakras?

What did your feet chakras look like? Was there much stagnant energy on the chakras?

Exercise: Distance Healing

You can also utilize the gingerbread man to work on others. When you performed the aura or aura/chakra clearing, you stood alongside your client working around her body, feeling and clearing the energy in her physical body, her aura and chakras. In this exercise, you will be sitting in a chair across from your client, looking and clearing any energy you may find. You can also use this technique when working with a client who is unable to come in person for a healing session, by performing a long distance healing.

In this next exercise, you will be using the same format as was described in the last exercise. If you need additional forms to practice on, there is a blank form in Appendix A, which you can use to make copies.

First prepare yourself for performing a reading.
Once prepared, say your client's name out loud three times.
On your reading screen, create a gauge and ask your client if she would like a healing. If the response you receive is yes, continue.
Then, ask yourself the following questions:
What does her gingerbread man look? Does it have two arms and legs, a head? Describe its physical appearance.

Grounding

Look at the gingerbread man's grounding cord on your reading screen.
Does the gingerbread man have a grounding cord? (Yes/No)

What does it look like?

Does it go all the way down to the center of the planet? (Yes/No)

Create a new grounding cord in present time.
Next, pretend that you have a handful of magic purple dust. Toss the
dust at its grounding cord.
What do you notice as you do this?
Using one of your psychic tools, clean off all the black dots.
Was there stagnant energy in your grounding cord? (Yes/No)

Where was it located?

The Aura
Look at the aura of the Gingerbread man on your reading screen.
What does it look like?
Does it go all the way around its body? (Yes/No)

Bring its aura down and around the gingerbread man's body, tucking it
into its grounding cord.
Toss the magic purple dust on its aura, watching as it turns black wher-
ever it finds stagnate energy.
Clean off all the black dots you find in its aura.

Did you find much stagnant energy in its aura? (Yes/No)

Was it in one area of the aura versus another? Please explain.

The Chakras

Look at each of her chakras on your reading screen.

Toss the magic purple dust on her first chakra with the intent that it will turn black wherever it finds stagnant energy.

Clean off all of the black dots from each chakra.

Record your observations.

What does her first chakra look like? Is there much stagnant energy on the chakra?

What does her second chakra look like? Is there much stagnant energy on the chakra?

What does her third chakra look like? Is there much stagnant energy on the chakra?

What does her fourth chakra look like? Is there much stagnant energy on the chakra?

What does her fifth chakra look like? Is there much stagnant energy on the chakra?

What does her sixth chakra look like? Is there much stagnant energy on the chakra?

What does her seventh chakra look like? Is there much stagnant energy on the chakra?

What does her hand chakras look like? Is there much stagnant energy on the chakras?

What do her feet chakra look like? Was there much stagnant energy on the chakras?

Take a moment to ask your client what she noticed as you performed the healing or how she feels now that the session is completed. Record her response.

Working With Issues

What Are Issues

We all have issues that we have chosen to work on in this lifetime. They are the thoughts, images and concepts that we view our lives through. They are our fears, our judgments, or beliefs that may not be in integrity with our true inner self. These energies can come from a number of places, including our upbringing, our present life experience or even from a past life.

Our issues may create a situation where our energy is not able to flow. We may find ourselves thinking one thing yet feeling another, or we may find ourselves unable to move forward in our lives because there is a subconscious block, which doesn't allow us to move in that direction.

This energy can lie in the aura, the chakras and the energy channels. The issue could have originated in a past life, where we brought it forward with us to this lifetime, causing us to relive it without understanding why or where it came from. At times the core to an issue can be so deep inside of us, we have covered over it with layer upon layer of other similar issues, thus creating new patterns of thoughts or behaviors. We become so out of touch with our true nature that we end up not understanding why we feel or behave in certain ways.

In this next section, you will have the opportunity to explore a number of tools that will assist you in looking at issues from a number of different perspectives. This is a very powerful section, but I think you will enjoy it immensely.

A Bouquet Of Roses

In this next technique, we will utilize the image of a rose to look at ourselves at a given moment in time. This non-judgmental tool allows you to observe your emotions and your progress in a cycle.

If you are open to receiving new energy or information, the rose will appear open, if not, the rose will appear closed. You can use this technique to look at where **you** were in the past, or in relationship to changes you are making in yourself now. You can also use this tool to look at other people's energy, either individually or together as a group. It is a quick and handy tool to use.

Exercise: Looking At Yourself As A Rose

In this next exercise, you will be looking at yourself in the form of a rose, and will be evaluating your relationship to your spiritual or intuitive information. Your information will appear as a ball of sphere of energy above your rose. Notice how your rose appears on your reading screen. Where is it in relationship to your information? Validate the feelings and impressions you are receiving as you look at yourself. Allow your consciousness to distinguish all of the details presented to you, and then draw a representation of that image below. Give yourself permission to create these roses to the best of your ability.

To begin, first prepare yourself for doing a reading, asking yourself "If I were a rose, what would I look like?"

On a separate sheet of paper, draw a picture of your rose. Add some amusement to this exercise. Try using crayons or colored pencils when drawing this image.

What does your rose look like?

What color is it?

What percent is it open or closed?

Is it standing or drooping?

Where is your rose in relationship to your information?

How do you feel as you look at your rose?

What else do you notice about the rose?

Exercise: Your Permission Rose

Permission is our ability to allow ourselves to be wherever we are at any given moment without judgment. This can be hard to do. Let's say for example, you have just come home after a hard day at work. You are tired, your muscles ache and you have a headache. Permission is all about allowing yourself a few minutes or even the whole evening to relax, to take a nap, a hot bath, or even to meditate.

Many of us don't give ourselves permission to have personal needs met. Instead, we push them aside, invalidate them and then charge ahead, washing the dishes, doing the laundry or cooking dinner. Permission is all about validating our feelings in the moment and then acting on those feelings, instead of denying, invalidating or judging them, only to turn around and beat ourselves up over them.

As you work on yourself or with clients, you will find that not many of us give ourselves permission to just "be". As you read this paragraph, do your find yourself going into judgment as to how you don't give yourself permission? Are you beating yourself up right now? Take this opportunity to say hello to the energy of self-judgment. Let it go. You are where you are right now and you will be where you will be tomorrow. Just let it go and "be". It is that simple.

In addition, while working with clients, also give them permission to be wherever they are at any moment. They are not you and there is no reason to judge where they are on their path. They are where they are supposed to be.

Take a moment to think about a situation in which you are currently involved. On your reading screen, have a sphere appear on the top of your screen that contains the energy of the situation. Create a rose that represents your ability to give yourself permission in this situation underneath the sphere. This is your permission rose. How much permission are you giving yourself? What else do you notice about this rose? Use the form in Appendix A to complete this exercise making copies of the form if needed.

Exercise: Your Neutrality Rose

When I speak of neutrality, I am speaking about non-judgment. It is our ability to look at and communicate information to others and ourselves without our own emotions getting in the way. We feel emotions in the second chakra and store our emotions in the fourth. We are in neutrality when we, as spirit, have our energy and attention above the fourth chakra, preferably in our Sacred Space.

It is essential when working with clients that we remain neutral while being in integrity with ourselves. When we speak from neutrality, we are not giving our opinion; we are just communicating what we are seeing. It is from this space that we relay information we may not agree with personally, or information that is emotionally charged.

Take a moment to think about a situation in which you are currently involved. On your reading screen, have a sphere appear on the top of your screen that contains your energy with regard to the situation. Create a rose that represents your ability to be neutral underneath the sphere. This is your neutrality rose. How neutral are you? What else do you notice about this rose? Use the form in Appendix A to complete this exercise making copies of the form if needed.

Exercise: Your Effort Rose

Effort implies that you are trying to hard too achieve something. When we do this, we use too much of our own personal energy. Instead of letting the thought, concept or situation go, letting the universe take care of it as she sees fit, we end up holding onto it for dear life. Instead of allowing it to do as it will, we smother it. The ironic thing about effort is that when we go into effort, nothing happens, so we try even harder, thus creating a snowball effect of useless effort. Sometimes we even go into effort trying to get out of effort.

On an energetic level, when we go into effort, the movement in the aura and the chakras begins to slow down, getting slower and slower as we pour more effort into it. One function of the chakras is to process our hopes and dreams. It is through the chakras that we allow them to manifest into the physical world. If they are slowed down or stopped, it makes it harder to bring things through and into the physical. The harder you try, the slower they go. If, on the other hand, you just let them go, stop trying or at least trying so hard, you can create the stuff of miracles.

Pick a topic, and take a moment to look at an effort rose. Have a sphere appear above your rose, which contains all of your effort. Where are you in relationship to your effort? What else do you notice about this rose? Make copies of the blank form in Appendix A to complete this exercise.

Exercise: Your Amusement Rose

Finding something funny about what you are doing

or a situation you are in is a great way to get your energy moving again. It is also a great tool to utilize when your energy is low, you are in effort, or you find yourself just plain stuck. By laughing at yourself or at what is going on around you, you create a shift in your own energy, raising it to a higher vibration, freeing up the energy that has stagnated in your aura and chakras.

As you continue to develop and work with your psychic abilities you will find times when you need to make a communication to your client that could be though of as being negative, threatening or even just unsavory. It is in theses situations, that I present the information to my client with humor. Though humor, your clients will get the communication. It will allow them to keep their energy flowing. It will keep them open to receiving the information as opposed to shutting down, which would end all potential communication.

Pick a situation that you are involved with now, and allow your amusement to appear as a rose, with the sphere containing the energy of the situation above it. Where is your amusement rose in relationship to the situation? What else do you notice about this rose? Make copies of the blank form in Appendix A to complete this exercise.

Exercise: A Rose Is A Rose Is A Rose

The energies described in the preceding exercises are only a few of the energies that you can look at using this technique. Energies such as fear, judgment and competition are a few others you may want to try. I'm sure there are a number of energies that you can think of right now that would also work well utilizing this technique. Take this opportunity to look at a few energies that come to mind, seeing your relationship to these energies in the form of a rose. Use a copy of the form in Appendix A to record your results.

Exercise: Looking At Other People's Energy As A Rose

Using this technique, you can also look at another

person's energy in the form of a rose. To do this, have your client sit before you as you have done in the past when performing a reading or healing. Next, prepare yourself for the session. On your reading screen, visualize a rose for that person with relationship to the sphere of her own information. Notice how easy it is to see. What does your client's rose look like? Where is it in relationship to her information?

As described before, you can also look different energies of another person in the form of a rose too. Try looking at a few different energies such as permission, neutrality, effort, amusement or a few of your own, recording your results on a copy of the form in Appendix A. At the end of each session, ask your client for any feedback they may have regarding the session.

Deprogramming

Over the years, we allow energy of one type or another to sit and stagnate in our aura, our chakras and even in the physical body. This can result in behavior patterns, wanted or unwanted, that we experience in our lives. When our life force energy stagnates in the physical, emotional, or spiritual bodies, it can manifest as physical problems, as well as life patterns and cycles that keep us from growing. In the physical body, this can appear in the form of headaches, back pain, arthritis, or cancer; in the emotional body, in the form of anger, rage, phobias, depression, and hate; and in the spiritual body as narrow-mindedness, disrespect for life and nature, or materialism. Once stagnated, we accept this energy as our own. These patterns can limit us from achieving our goals, from being who we want to be.

Removing specific stagnant energy from the physical, emotional and spiritual body is called deprogramming. Deprogramming is another simple technique to master. By tossing magic purple dust into the aura, you can easily see where the energy of that issue has stagnated in the aura and body. You can use it to deprogram your own issues as well as issues your clients may have.

Exercise: Deprogramming A Client

To begin, first have your client select an issue or behavior that she would like to release.

Sitting across from your client, prepare yourself to perform a reading.

As you sit with your eyes closed, pretend you have a handful of magic purple dust.

Toss the purple dust onto your client with the intent that it will stick to the energy of the issue in your client's aura or on her physical body.

Watch as the magic purple dust lands on your client's body, observing as it turns into little black dots when it lands on energy has stagnated.

Communicate to your client where you see the black dots sitting in and on her body.

Using your hand, a feather duster, a squeegee or any other psychic tool, remove the black dots from her body.

Communicate any impressions you get or anything you may feel as you are working.

Once all of the black dots are removed, repeat the process of tossing magic purple dust on your client until the purple dust no longer sticks to her body.

Call back your clients, energy filling her bodies the energy of her highest good.

Practice this technique using the different energies noted below. Record your observations.

Effort

Deprogram the effort your client goes into when she is trying to create for herself.

Where does the effort sit in her body?

Is it more concentrated in one area than another? Describe where.

What else do you see, feel or notice when you work on removing effort from her space?

Ask your client what she noticed after you removed this energy from her space.

Permission

Deprogram the invalidation in your client. Where doesn't she give herself permission?

Where does the non-permission rest in her body?

Is it more concentrated in one area than another? Describe where.

What else do you see, feel or notice when you work on removing invalidation from her space?

Ask your client what she noticed after you removed this energy from her space.

Neutrality

Deprogram any energy that keeps your client from being in neutrality. Where does judgment rest in her body?

Is it more concentrated in one area than another? Describe where.

What else do you see, feel or notice when you work on removing judgment out of her space making more room for neutrality?

Ask your client what she noticed after you removed this energy from her space.

Looking At Issues In The Aura

Up until this point, you have experienced working with the aura, the electromagnetic field around the body in generic ways. You have learned to feel and clear your aura and the aura of others, you have also learned how to look at where the aura is around the body, as well as were in the aura we carry specific energies.

The aura, however, is the place in which we carry our pictures so that we can process them. When look through these pictures they create our reality of the world around us. I find it interesting when performing a clairsentient healing such as an aura/chakra clearing on a client that it is hard, if not impossible to look at the pictures in the aura if I am standing inside his or her aura. I find that if I want to look at the underlying picture they are holding on to is, I need to take a step back out of their space, so that I can see it.

In turn, it is very difficult to look at the same kinds of pictures in your own aura, because you exist in the middle of your own space. Other than your own judgments, invalidation or denial of the energy, we carry the picture so close to the body they are just plain hard to look at. For this reason, in this section, we will only be looking at the energy others carry around in their auras.

The aura is made up of seven distinct layers, with the first layer being closest to the body and the seventh layer the furthest away. The energies carried in the aura correspond to the energies processed in the chakras. For example, the first chakra processes our survival information, while we carry our survival pictures in the first layer of the aura. The only exception to this rule are the sixth and seventh layers or the aura, where for simplicity of the reading, we will look at how your client sees the world (sixth layer) and how the world sees your client (seventh layer).

In this next exercise, you will be looking at each layer of the aura, describing the layer first as a color and then looking underneath that energetic vibration to look at the picture(s) your client carries there. As you do this exercise, take the time to dissipate as much energy as is required to see the pictures in your client's aura.

It is especially true when reading the aura that the pictures you see can and will seem far out to you, as if you are making it up. Trust that the information you are receiving is true. Communicate it to your client without judgment or editing. Just because it doesn't make sense to you doesn't mean it won't vibrate as truth to them.

Exercise: Reading The Aura

In this exercise, you will be looking at each layer of your client's aura. First identify at what color the layer is vibrating. Then look into the color of that layer and communicate to your client what she is creating for herself. Use the definition below to help you identify what kinds of pictures she is carrying in each of the different layers. This will aid you in phrasing your questions to yourself. Use whatever additional tools you need to assist you in this communication.

In the space provided below, record the color of each layer and what pictures you observe in that layer.

First Layer–*Grounding, Survival, Physical Body*
Color:

Second Layer–*Clairsentience, Desires, Sexuality, Creativity*
Color:

Third Layer–*Power, Will Power, Energy, Motivation*
Color:

Fourth Layer–*Affinity, Unconditional love*
Color:

Fifth Layer–*Communication*
Color:

Sixth Layer–*How she sees the world*
Color:

Seventh Layer–*How the world sees her*
Color:

Looking At The Past

We are all spirits, living in a physical body and have existed since the beginning of time. We choose to incarnate in the physical so that we can learn how to live and function on this planet and in this reality. We have also lived and existed at many other times, on this planet, on other planets and in other parallel realities.

Like ourselves, others have chosen to live and learn in this universe, in this reality. With each lifetime, we choose the people with whom we wish to interact and the lessons we come here to learn. It is possible for us to look at the lifetimes we have lived and shared with others.

In this next exercise we will get to look at our past, our past lives that is. Try this technique out on yourself and then try it on a friend or a client, using copies of the form in Appendix A.

Exercise: Discovering A Past Life

Prepare yourself for a reading.

On your reading screen, visualize the Earth. It can appear to be rotating in space, or you can see it as a globe spinning in its stand.

Give the Earth a grounding cord that goes to the center of the Milky Way and set it on release.

As you look at the Earth spinning before you, allow a little red dot to appear any place where you have had a past life.

As you watch the Earth passing in front of you, you may see that some of the red dots are brighter than others.

Pick one of these places.

Take a deep breath.

From your vantage point outside the Earth, allow your consciousness to go into the bright red dot, filling your awareness with the energy of the location you picked, going back to the time in which you lived there.

Dissipate any resistance energy that you may be encountering.

Take one more deep breath and look around you.

Where are you? What country did you select?

What year or time period is it? What do you look like in this lifetime? Were you male, female, your or old?

What were you doing in this lifetime?

Did you see anyone else there? What do they look like?

What is your relationship to them?

What kind of interactions are you having with them?

How do you feel as you have these interactions?

Why you have chosen to look at this lifetime?

What information are you utilizing in this lifetime that you gained from that past life?

Getting Your Buttons Pushed

When we interact with people in our daily lives, we sometimes get what is euphemistically called, "our buttons pushed". When our buttons are pushed, we respond with feelings of pain, anger, guilt or fear. Many of us blame the button pusher for making us feel a certain way. But what is really going on?

There have been many times in our lives where we have been called stupid, ugly or some other invalidating term. I find it interesting that in some instances, the comment, statement or action has no impact on us. It just rolls off our backs. In other instances, we allow the energy to stick. Our buttons get pushed and we respond to this energy, turning around and blaming the other person. What we don't see is that it was, and always will be, our choice to hold onto, or react to, this energy.

The question I would like to propose is: what is the underlying energy or issue that causes us to react or respond in a certain way. Infants, for example, who are first learning to walk will fall on their knees, bump into furniture or even hit their heads. If left alone, they will right themselves and continue on their merry way. Unless their tumble was severe, they will not and do not cry. They let the energy, the experience of falling flow right through them. It is not until we teach our children that there is something to be concerned about when they fall that they allow the seed to be planted. Some children also learn they will get attention after hurting themselves. We are the ones who teach our children how to have energy stick in their bodies.

Boulders

Let's look at this concept from another perspective. Visualize your life force energy as a fast moving stream. It will flow in the path of least resistance. If a large stone is placed in the center of the stream, the water must yield and deviate to go around the stone blocking its path. The flow of the stream has deviated from its natural path and become imbalanced.

If, the first time you felt invalidated, a large stone was placed in the stream, the effect to the flow of energy may not be great. However, if you are invalidated again, the blockage can get bigger as yet another stone is added. Your life force energy must yield and deviate even more to get around the even larger blockage. These blockages can grow instance-by-instance, cycle-by-cycle, stone after stone, creating buttons that anyone can push in your space.

We can all learn how to "unplug" the issues in our lives. Unblock the river or remove the buttons that hinder us. To remove a button, we must first find its core, the place where it all started, the first rock that was thrown or the seed. For many of us, the stream is full of so many rocks and boulders; it may take a while for us to remove them all. For others, they may be sick of the river being blocked and will employ drastic means to remove the buttons like energetic dynamite. There are others who have been working on clearing the river for some time and they are ready to let go of and release that last rock. Wherever you are, give yourself permission to be there.

Onions

As we build up energies or issues in our physical, emotional or spiritual bodies, we store these experiences like the layers of an onion. In this next exercise, we will begin to unveil the onion. Give yourself permission to not get to the core on the first try. It took you years to build this onion, allow yourself a little time to take it apart. As you do this exercise, you may experience a picture or even just a color with an associated feeling. Trust your feelings. Look behind the outer layer of the onion to the layer below it, continuing on looking at each successive layer until you experience oneness with yourself.

Also note, there are many times as we unravel the onion that we get to a point in which we experience the feeling of oneness. We have reached a point in the unfolding that there was a major shift in our energy. It's like someone who is accustomed to being abused and they find the core picture for that situation and why it keeps repeating in their life. While they will probably experience this as a major shift in their world, there is probably more energy sitting behind that revelation that was the original cause for bringing on the abuse in the first place. After completing this exercise, give yourself a bit of time to process all the changes you have just made in your space. Then you may want to go back and check to see if you have removed the whole thing or just a part of it.

While the results of this exercise are similar to deprogramming, in this exercise you get to look at each of the underlying energies involved. This is beneficial when working in a reading space versus a healing space where communication of the pictures and issues tends to be minimal. While this exercise is directed toward working on yourself, you can also utilize this technique with a client.

Exercise: Getting Down To The Core Of The Issue

To begin, sit in a comfortable straight-backed chair and prepare yourself for doing a reading.

Say hello to your body.

Send loving and healing thoughts to yourself as you go through this exercise.

Create a gauge in front of yourself and look at how much permission you are giving yourself to be wherever you might be as you perform this exercise.

Give your permission gauge a grounding cord and allow any non-permission energy to drain off of it.

Look to see if the amount of permission you are giving yourself has gone up.

Validate yourself for any change you notice.

Now, pick an issue you would like to work on.

That's right, the first thing that comes to mind.

Say hello to that picture.

Say hello to any feelings that the picture invokes in you.

Notice how it makes your body feel.

Where in your body do you notice this energy?

Does it vibrate at a certain color?

What color is it?

Or is it a scene from your life?

Just look at it, validate it, and give yourself permission to look at it.

Dissipate any emotional energy you may be experiencing until you find yourself comfortable with this image.

Now, pretend that the image you see on your reading screen is just a two dimensional picture and that you can turn back the pages in a book called "My Life".

Turn the page back.

Without judgment, look at what is under the original picture.

What do you see?

Notice if your feelings change as you look at this new picture.

Dissipate any energy as required so that you become comfortable with this new image.

Say hello to your amusement.

Again, flip back another page.

What do you see and feel here?

Dissipate any energy from your space that is keeping your from seeing the page.

Continue this process until you experience a feeling of oneness, or wholeness as spirit.

Take a deep breath.

Notice what it feels like to be in a space of wholeness once again.

Love yourself for being able to give yourself this space.

Finally, summon your energy of this issue back that you.

Remember, you left some of your energy in all of these places.

Have it fill your physical, emotional and spiritual bodies.

Feel good with having your energy back.

When you are feeling refreshed, revitalized and clear, open your eyes and stretch your body.

What issue did you choose to work on?

How many layers did you work though until you found a place of contentment?

Where in your body was this energy located?

Describe the pictures you found as you worked through this issue. How did you feel as you looked at these pictures?

How do you feel now that you have cleared the energy related to this issue?

What else do you or did you notice as you did this exercise?

Exercise: Getting Down To The Core Of A Client's Issue

Prepare yourself for doing a reading.

Create a gauge in front of you and look at how much permission you are giving yourself to look at the energy of your client's issues.

Give your permission gauge a grounding cord and allow any non-permission energy to drain off of it.

Look to see if the amount of permission you are giving yourself has gone up.

Validate yourself for any change you notice.

Now, ask your client to pick an issue that she would like for you to look at for her.

What is your client's issue?

At what color does her issue vibrate?

Look behind this color and say hello to any images this color invokes in you.

Dissipate any energy you may be experiencing until you find yourself comfortable looking at this image.

What is the picture you are being shown?

How does this picture impact your client on physical, emotional or spiritual levels?

Communicate your observations to your client.

*Clear your client of the effects this energy is having on her using what-
ever tool seems appropriate.*

*Next, pretend, that the image you see on your reading screen is just a
two dimensional picture and that you can turn back the pages in a
book.*

Turn the page back.

Without judgment, look at what is under the original picture.

*Dissipate any energy as required so that you become comfortable with
this image.*

What do you see?

Is it a new color or picture?

Describe what you see now.

How does this picture impact your client on physical, emotional or
spiritual levels?

Communicate this information to your client.

*Clear your client of the effects of this energy using whatever tool seems
appropriate.*

Again, flip back another page.

What do you see and feel here?

*Continue this process until you feel that your client has reached a place
of oneness, or wholeness as spirit.*

Have your client take a deep breath.

*Ask them to take a moment to notice what it feels like to be into this
space of wholeness once again.*

Finally, summon your client's energy of this issue back to her.

Have it fill her physical, emotional and spiritual bodies.
Tell her that when she is feeling refreshed, revitalized and clear, she can get up and stretch her body.

Looking Deeper Into The Body

Kinesthetic

Kinesthetic, while not a "psychic" ability associated with a specific chakra, is a great tool to use when working with clients on deeper healing levels. When your body is experiencing energy on kinesthetic levels, it reflects the pain or trauma in your client's body.

There have been many occasions when sitting across from a client, that I will find a spot in my body starting to throb or get hot or will find myself with a low grade headache or stomachache.

Let's say for example that I feel a throbbing sensation in the middle of my right calf. As I acknowledge the feeling in my body, I will always ask my client "What did you do to your left leg?" and point to the spot on my body that hurts. (Remember, it is mirroring the energy, so if you are sitting across from your client, the sensations will always be reversed in her body). 99.9% of the time, you will find that there is or had been an issue or trauma that affected the part of your client's body you identified.

I find that by acknowledging this energy in my body, I have a wonderful diagnostic tool to work with. The sensation of pain, heat or discomfort that you experience in your body during a session will always go away as you move your energy and attention away from that part of your client's body or they move out your physical proximity.

While this technique or concept may sound strange, try to

incorporate it into your next reading or healing session. Check in with your body, validating any aches or pains you may be experiencing. Then ask your client about them. I think you will be truly amazed by the results.

Medical Intuition

Disease, when looked at clairvoyantly, takes on specific shapes and sizes in the muscles, glands and organs of the physical body as well as in the aura and chakras of the energetic body. All diseases carry distinct energetic patterns that are instantly discernible to a keen psychic observer or medical intuitive.

When people think of disease, they think of things like Cancer or heart disease. They recall Aunt Fanny who had a malignant tumor removed due to cancer or Uncle Frank who just had triple by-pass surgery done, due to hardening of the arteries. Modern medicine has taught us to look for a name or label to associate with health conditions.

Medical intuition doesn't work that way. Instead of labeling, medical intuitives look at the body on energetic levels. An intuitive might see inflammation in a body part, notice an imbalance in the functioning of an organ or gland, or validate a strong emotion that has been left unresolved for a long time. They look for the imbalanced physiological, mental or emotional energies and sometimes receive back a whole lot more information.

Medical intuition operates on this basic principle: If you ask a question, you will always receive an answer back.

I would like to take a moment to emphasis one critical point. As a healer, you are unable to *directly cure* an individual of disease. Instead, your role is to help *facilitate the healing* of individuals so that they can let go of stagnant energy that keeps them out of balance and in a state of illness. As a psychic, you must remember that you are not a medical doctor. You cannot, therefore diagnose, treat, alleviate, mitigate, prevent or care for any disease of any kind, in anyway. Period.

Issues Of The Physical Body

When looked at energetically, the cause of all disease is a holding onto energy within the physical, emotional and spiritual bodies that is not in harmony with us. Healing is experienced as a letting go of disharmonious energy. An individual can choose to hang on to the issue(s) that are causing the disease, or they can choose to let it go. It is this letting go that can dramatically reduce the symptoms of the disease, or potentially cure the individual of the disease.

For example, I once had with a client who came for a reading. When she sat down in front of me I noticed an accumulation of stagnant energy sitting on and around her fourth chakra, her heart center. I commented to my client about the energy I saw and told her that there were a number of unresolved issues regarding her mother. Immediately, she informed me that it couldn't be true, because she never knew her birth mother, in that she had been put up for adoption as an infant. She went on to tell me that she had just had quadruple bypass-pass surgery. I chuckled inside, as I watched this woman sit in denial of the real cause of her disease.

Below is a description of the energetic pattern of a few diseases that afflict millions of Americans each year. As you continue working with clients, I am sure that you will be able find and identify the energetics of many other diseases and what they look like in the physical body.

Multiple Sclerosis

Multiple Sclerosis (MS) has been *medically* diagnosed as a neurological disorder. *Energetically*, it appears as if electrical wires (the nerves) have been cut and are flailing around like fire hoses with no one at the control. These energy patterns appear where individuals are manifesting the disease in their body. For example, if your client is having problems with their vision and speech, the nerves would appear cut in the head and neck area. If they are having problems walking, the nerves will appear to be cut in the back or legs.

Lupus

Lupus, also a diagnosed as a neurological disorder, has a similar look and feel to MS. In the body, however, Lupus energetically appears as if the nerves are giant rubber bands stretching and moving, almost with a life of their own. There is no "tension" to the nerves and individuals with this disorder often feel as if they have little or no control over their muscular functions.

Parkinson's Disease

Parkinson's Disease is also medically classified as a neurological disorder. Unlike the cut or flailing nerves of MS or the non-control of Lupus, individuals with Parkinson's disease have a characteristic area of what appears to be inflammation in the mid-brain. In these individuals, signs of this disease can also appear in the body as if the muscles of the arms and legs are in constant contraction. It is this contraction that causes the extremities, i.e. the hands and feet, to shake. Try contracting the muscles of your arms and hold them as tight as possible. Look to see if your hands start to shake. This is the energetics of Parkinson's disease.

Chronic Fatigue Syndrome (CFS)

Some diseases, such as Chronic Fatigue Syndrome (CFS), energetically appear external to the physical body and is typically seen attached to, or in close proximity to a chakra. Although CFS can affect the person as a whole, the affects seem to come and go. The affects are first felt in the area of the chakra that it is affected and then moves through the rest of the body from that location. For example, if the seventh chakra is affected, the person will typically first feel confused, dizzy, have blurred vision or have confused mental processes. If, on the other hand, the fourth chakra is affected, the individual will tend to experience the affect of the CFS in the lower parts of the body, feeling tired or worn out, while mental activity is not impaired.

Acquired Immune Deficiency Syndrome (AIDS)

Acquired Immune Deficiency Syndrome (AIDS), on the other hand, does not appear in the muscles, glands or organs of the physical body nor does it appear in association with a chakra. Instead, it appears in the aura as a degradation of the aura. When seen energetically, the aura of an individual with AIDS is typically seen as being yellow to yellow-brown in color and lacks in luster. When the disease moves into its more advanced state, the aura appears to have developed holes or looks as if it is disintegrating. With the natural protection of the aura compromised, individuals with AIDS are energetically more susceptible to contracting contagious illnesses.

An In-depth Look At Chakras

As discussed earlier, chakras are energy centers within the body that open and close like the apertures of a camera. When looked at clairvoyantly, a healthy chakra should be clear in color and full of energy. They should be one to two inches in diameter, about the size of a silver dollar. A healthy chakra should appear free of stagnant energy and should rotate in a clockwise direction.

There are two distinct sections to a chakra. The outer section is a band that runs along the outside edge of the chakra and the spinning center. The outer band is what controls the opening and closing of the chakra. This band works like a muscle. The center section of the chakra is what processes the information.

Each chakra spins at a different speed or frequency starting slowly in the first chakra and increasing in speed as you move through the body to the seventh chakra. Maybe it should be expressed that the chakras are actually slowing down energy and information as you move from the etheric through the body into the density of the physical world.

Chakras can also be likened to a plate, and like all things that exist in our three-dimensional world; it has at least two sides. Chakras also collect and accumulate energy on and around them. I'm sure you experienced this earlier as you worked through many of the exercises in this book.

The chakras exist inside the body and lie along the front of the spine. Associated with the chakras are the chakra vortexes or nadis that quite literally funnel energy. These vortexes stick out and away from the body and through the aura, attaching to each layer of the aura where the vortex and aura intersect. It is through these vortexes that we receive information from the world around us. The information comes down and through the funnel and is processed by the chakra.

As you continue to develop your psychic abilities and work more with the energy of the chakras, remember to check and clear both sides of it. The vortexes should be straight and clear of any stagnant energy. In addition, ensure that there is not any energy sitting over the opening of the vortex, blocking information from coming in.

Chakra Ailments

Our chakras also reflect ailments and issues we are working on. Although listed separately, chakras can take on one or all of the problems listed below.

Stagnant Energy On Chakra

When energy has stagnated on a chakra, it can block or reduce the amount of information that can be processed. This energy will appear as being dark in color or black. Stagnant energy can appear on any portion or can completely cover the chakra. Some chakras may even have a thin film of energy that completely covers the whole chakra. This tends to cause the chakra to filter all of the information it encounters. Others may only have a section of the chakra covered with stagnant energy.

Stagnant energy can also vary in density. Energy that appears dense typically indicates that it has been sitting there for a long time. It's like dirty dishes that have been sitting on the counter overnight. When you try to clean them, the dirt has grown harder and denser and more difficult to get off. Less dense energy is usually easier to remove.

Outer Band Of Chakra Locked

Have you ever had the situation where you were walking across the street or even driving your car and you were almost hit? Immediately, you body responded. It is because your first chakra opened up. For some people, however, energy has accumulated and fixated the outer band of their chakra, which makes it impossible for the chakra to open and close. This can make the individual rigid, rigid of body, mind or spirit. They may even experience this as tightness in the physical body.

Cracked Chakras

Chakras, especially the chakras of the hands and feet can appear cracked. Typically, the damage to the chakra appears in the outer band, but I have seen cracks go all the way to the center of the chakra. Cracks also have depth and some cracks can be very deep. Many individuals who have tendentious or carpal tunnel syndrome have cracked hand chakra, while individuals with sore or numb feet or even bad circulation have cracked feet chakra.

Chakras That Are Not Rotating

For whatever reason, chakras can also stop rotating, thus they are not processing any information. The chakra is stuck and individuals may experience the feeling of being stuck in their daily lives.

Chakras That Are Rotating Backwards

Chakras can also rotate in a counter clockwise direction. While the chakra is not stuck and unmoving, it is also not processing information correctly. This sometimes is seen when people can only give of themselves and cannot receive. This issue can also seen in individuals who want and try to be different or even people who are trying very hard to break away from a specific thought or convention.

Backed-up Chakras

When a chakra is not functioning properly, energy can build up around the chakra. The accumulated energy can become so large that it can impact the next chakra in alignment. For example, let's say that your third chakra, or power space, is backed up, resulting in an inability for you to use your power for yourself. This inability, over time, can create a serious blockage in your energetic system. If the blockage continues to grow, the fourth chakra, our heart center, can become impacted. While the issue did not start in the fourth chakra, once it is impacted by stagnant energy from the third, it will too begin to malfunction and lose its ability to process information.

Flattened Chakras

Chakras may also appear as being flattened or oblong in shape. Many times if individuals are experiencing pressure or stress in their lives, they will have this condition. When seen, this issue will usually impact all of their chakras and will also impact the rotation of the chakra because it is unable to rotate correctly.

Chakras Out Of Alignment

Chakras can also appear out of alignment. Chakras should appear in line through the body. When a chakra is knocked out of alignment, there is typically an issue keeping it out of balance. The misaligned chakra, although it may still be processing information, is not in communication with the rest of the energetic system.

First and Seventh Chakra Blocked

We receive information and energy into our bodies via the seventh chakra. It travels through the body and is finally manifested into the physical via the first chakra. Some individuals who feel stuck have their first and seventh chakras blocked, leaving them feeling confused or out of touch with their own information. These individuals may also be experiencing problems dealing and working in the physical world, having difficulties making decisions or taking their next step.

Distorted Chakra Vortexes

Some issues can block the functioning of the chakra vortexes. The vortexes can be crooked or lopsided causing the information to be distorted. The vortexes can also stick out further on one side of the body or the other, creating an imbalance to how the chakra is processing information by being over stimulated in one area and not enough in the other. An example of this is when the second chakra (the chakra of feeling and nurturing) sticks out in front causing us to give and nurture others while it is pushed in the back, which does not allow us to give to ourselves.

Putting It All Together

Clairvoyant Reading And Healing

In this section, we will be putting everything we have covered together. The questions given are to be used as a guideline. Feel free to add any additional questions that may come to mind as you do these exercises. You can also utilize any of the tools and techniques we have covered throughout this book to assist you in performing the clairvoyant reading and healing that follow. As you go through each of the questions and look at the different energies, communicate what you see to your client.

Exercise: Clairvoyant Healing

Below is an outline you can follow while performing a Clairvoyant Healing. When performing a healing I find it difficult to fill out a form and work with energy at the same time. It is for this reason, this exercise is in format you see. It is to be used as a reminder of the steps involved when performing a clairvoyant healing. Do not feel limited to only asking these questions of yourself or your client.

Grounding
What does her grounding cord look like?
Does it go all the way down to the center of the planet?

Is it set on release? If no, what energy that is keeping her from grounding.

Are there any cords going into her grounding cord? If yes, why are the cords there?

Create a new grounding cord for your client. Set it on release.

Body/Being

Where is your client, as spirit, in relationship to her body?

If she is not in her body, what energy is keeping her out of it?

When was she knocked her out of her body. Why?

Move your client, as spirit, back into her body, aligning any chakras as required.

The Aura

What does your client's aura look like?

Does their aura go all the way around her body?

Where is her aura in relationship to her body?

Move her aura around her body and tuck it into her grounding cord. Set her aura on release.

The Chakras

Look at each of your client's chakras. Starting at her first chakra, look at and clear each of the seven major chakras. Then clear each of the chakra in her hands and feet.

What color is her _____ chakra?

What is the issue(s) is she processing in this chakra?

Are there any cords going into this chakra? How do they impact your client?

Is there any energy in this chakra that needs to be cleared?

What else do I notice about this chakra?

Clear any unwanted energy and repair any damage you may find in that chakra.

Earth Energy

Look to see if your client's earth energy is flowing?

What color is flowing through her leg channels?

Is there any stagnant energy that needs to be cleared from these channels?

Clear any stagnant energy that you may find.

Assist your client in bringing some energy in from Mother Earth.

Universal Energy

Look to see if your client's universal energy is flowing?

What color is flowing through her back channels?

Is there any stagnant energy that needs to be cleared?

Clear any stagnant energy that you may find.

Assist your client in bring universal energy down her back channels and up the front channels.

Healing Energy

Look to see if your client's energy is flowing?

What color is flowing through her arm channels?

Is there any stagnant energy that needs to be cleared?

Clear any unwanted energy that you may find.

Bring energy from your client's fourth chakra through her arms and out her hands.

Questions

Allow your client to ask you a few questions of her own.

Question:

Question:

Question:

Exercise: Clairvoyant Reading

Looking At Your Client As A Rose

On a separate sheet of paper, draw a picture of your client in the image of a rose in relationship to her own spiritual information. What does her rose look like?

What color is it? Is there any significance to the color?

What percent is it open or closed?

Is it standing or drooping?

Where is her rose in relationship to her information?

How do you feel as you look at her rose?

What else do you notice about the rose?

Past Life Reading

In this section, we will be taking a moment to look a few of your client's past lives.

At what color does this past life vibrate?

Where is she in this lifetime? (i.e. what country)

What year or time period is it?

What does she look like in this lifetime? Was she male of female, young or old?

What is she doing in this lifetime?

Do you see anyone else there? What do they look like?

What is his/her relationship to your client?

What kind of interactions are they having? How do you feel as you observe these interactions?

Why has she chosen to look at this lifetime?

What information is she utilizing in this lifetime that she gained from this past life?

Looking At Chakras

In this section, take a look at each of her chakras.

First Chakra
       Survival   %

Second Chakra
       Clairsentience/Desires   %
       Desire/Creativity   %

Third Chakra
       Power, Energy   %
       Out of Body Experience   %
       Out of Body Memory   %

Fourth Chakra
       Affinity   %

Fifth Chakra
       Clairaudience   %
       Inner Voice   %
       Telepathy   %
       Pragmatic Intuition   %

Sixth Chakra
       Clairvoyance   %
       Abstract Intuition   %

Seventh Chakra
       Trance Mediumship/Body   %
       Trance Mediumship/Being   %

Knowingness   %

Hand Chakra, Left   %

Hand Chakra, Right   %

Foot Chakra, Left   %

Foot Chakra, Right   %

Looking At The Aura

Next, take a look at each layer of her aura, identifying at what color the layer is vibrating, then communicate to your client what she is creating for herself.

First Layer–*Grounding, Survival, Physical Body*
Color:

Second Layer–*Clairsentience, Desires, Sexuality, Creativity*
Color:

Third Layer–*Power, Will Power, Energy, Motivation*
Color:

Fourth Layer–*Affinity, Unconditional love*
Color:

Fifth Layer–*Communication*
Color:

Sixth Layer–*How she sees the world*
Color:

Seventh Layer–*How the world sees her*
Color:

Questions

Allow your client to ask you a few questions of her own.

Question:

Question:

Question:

Appendix

A Simple Energy Check

Grounding

What does her grounding cord look like?

How long is it? (Does it go all the way to the center of the planet?)

Is her grounding cord releasing energy? (Yes/No)

Is her grounding cord in present time? (Yes/No)

The Aura

Where is her aura in relationship to her body?

Does it go all the way around the body, including around her feet? (Yes/No)

Does her aura tuck into her grounding cord? (Yes/No)

Is her aura set on release? (Yes/No)

The Chakras

Starting at your client's first chakra, create a gauge and ask yourself: How much is she utilizing the energy of her first chakra?

How much is she utilizing the energy of her second chakra?

How much is she utilizing the energy of her third chakra?

How much is she utilizing the energy of her fourth chakra?

How much is she utilizing the energy of her fifth chakra?

How much is she utilizing the energy of her sixth chakra?

How much is she utilizing the energy of her seventh chakra?

Questions
Question/Percentage:

Question/Percentage:

Question/Percentage:

Question/Percentage:

Distance Healing

General Observation
What does her gingerbread man look? Does it have two arms and legs, a head? Describe its physical appearance.

Grounding
Look at the gingerbread man's grounding cord on your reading screen.
Does the gingerbread man have a grounding cord? (Yes/No)

What does it look like?

Does it go all the way down to the center of the planet? (Yes/No)

Was there stagnant energy in your grounding cord? (Yes/No)

Where was it located?

The Aura
Look at the aura of the Gingerbread man on your reading screen.
What does it look like?

Does it go all the way around its body? (Yes/No)

Did you find much stagnant energy in its aura? (Yes/No)

Was it in one area of the aura versus another? Please explain.

The Chakras

Look at each of her chakras on your reading screen.

What does her first chakra look like? Is there much stagnant energy on the chakra?

What does her second chakra look like? Is there much stagnant energy on the chakra?

What does her third chakra look like? Is there much stagnant energy on the chakra?

What does her fourth chakra look like? Is there much stagnant energy on the chakra?

What does her fifth chakra look like? Is there much stagnant energy on the chakra?

What does her sixth chakra look like? Is there much stagnant energy on the chakra?

What does her seventh chakra look like? Is there much stagnant energy on the chakra?

What does her hand chakras look like? Is there much stagnant energy on the chakras?

What do her feet chakra look like? Was there much stagnant energy on the chakras?

Take a moment to ask your client what she noticed as you performed the healing or how she feels now that the session is completed. Record her response.

Looking At Roses

On a separate sheet of paper, draw a picture of your client's
_____ *rose. Add some amusement to this exercise.*
Try using crayons or colored pencils when drawing this image.
What does her rose look like?

What color is it? Is there any significance to the color?

What percent is it open or closed?

Is it standing or drooping?

Where is her rose in relationship to your information?

How do you feel as you look at her rose?

What else do you notice about her rose?

Deprogramming

Have your client select an energy she would like deprogrammed.

Where does the energy sit in her body?

Is it more concentrated in one area than another? Describe where.

What else do you see, feel or notice when you work on removing this energy from her space?

Ask your client what she noticed after you removed this energy from her space.

Getting Down To The Core Of A Client's Issue

Ask your client to pick an issue that she would like for you to look at for her.
What is your client's issue?

At what color does her issue vibrate?

Look behind this color and say hello to any images this color invokes in you.
What is the picture you are being shown?

How does this picture impact your client on physical, emotional or spiritual levels?

Communicate your observations to your client.
Turn the page back.
Describe what you see now.
How does this picture impact your client on physical, emotional or spiritual levels?

Communicate this information to you client.
Again, flip back another page.
Continue this process until you feel that your client has reached a place of oneness, or wholeness of spirit.

A Clairvoyant Healing

Grounding

What does her grounding cord look like?

Does it go all the way down to the center of the planet?

Is it set on release? If no, what energy that is keeping her from grounding.

Are there any cords going into her grounding cord? If yes, why are the cords there?

Create a new grounding cord for your client. Set it on release.

Body/Being

Where is your client, as spirit, in relationship to her body?

If she is not in her body, what energy is keeping her out of it?

When was she knocked her out of her body. Why?

Move your client, as spirit, back into her body, aligning any chakras as required.

The Aura

What does your client's aura look like?

Does their aura go all the way around her body?

Where is her aura in relationship to her body?

Move her aura around her body and tuck it into her grounding cord. Set her aura on release.

The Chakras

Look at each of your client's chakras. Starting at her first chakra, look at and clear each of the seven major chakras. Then clear each of the chakra in her hands and feet.

What color is her _____ chakra?

What is the issue(s) is she processing in this chakra?

Are there any cords going into this chakra? How do they impact your client?

Is there any energy in this chakra that needs to be cleared?

What else do I notice about this chakra?

Clear any unwanted energy and repair any damage you may find in this chakra.

Earth Energy

Look to see if your client's earth energy is flowing?
What color is flowing through her leg channels?
Is there any stagnant energy that needs to be cleared from these channels?
Clear any stagnant energy that you may find.
Assist your client in bringing some energy in from Mother Earth.

Universal Energy

Look to see if your client's universal energy is flowing?
What color is flowing through her back channels?
Is there any stagnant energy that needs to be cleared?
Clear any stagnant energy that you may find.
Assist your client in bring universal energy down her back channels
and up the front channels.

Healing Energy

Look to see if your client's energy is flowing?
What color is flowing through her arm channels?
Is there any stagnant energy that needs to be cleared?
Clear any unwanted energy that you may find.
Bring energy from your client's fourth chakra through her arms and
out her hands.

Questions

Allow your client to ask you a few questions of her own.
Question:

Question:

Question:

A Clairvoyant Reading

Looking At Your Client As A Rose

On a separate sheet of paper, draw a picture of your client in the image of a rose in relationship to her own spiritual information.

What does her rose look like?

What color is it? Is there any significance to the color?

What percent is it open or closed?

Is it standing or drooping?

Where is her rose in relationship to her information?

How do you feel as you look at her rose?

What else do you notice about the rose?

Past Life Reading

In this section, we will be taking a moment to look a few of your client's past lives.

At what color does this past life vibrate?

Where is she in this lifetime? (i.e. what country)

What year or time period is it?

What does she look like in this lifetime? Was she male of female, young or old?
What is she doing in this lifetime?

Do you see anyone else there? What do they look like?

What is his/her relationship to your client?

What kind of interactions are they having?

How do you feel as you observe these interactions?

Why has she chosen to look at this lifetime?

What information is she utilizing in this lifetime that she gained from this past life?

Looking At Chakras

In this section, take a look at each of her chakras.

First Chakra
    Survival   %

Second Chakra

     Clairsentience/Desires   %

     Desire/Creativity   %

Third Chakra

     Power, Energy   %

     Out of Body Experience   %

     Out of Body Memory   %

Fourth Chakra

     Affinity   %

Fifth Chakra

     Clairaudience   %

     Inner Voice   %

     Telepathy   %

     Pragmatic Intuition   %

Sixth Chakra

     Clairvoyance   %

     Abstract Intuition   %

Seventh Chakra

     Trance Mediumship/Body   %

     Trance Mediumship/Being   %

Knowingness   %

Hand Chakra, Left   %

Hand Chakra, Right   %

Foot Chakra, Left   %

Foot Chakra, Right   %

Looking At The Aura

Next, take a look at each layer of her aura, identifying at what color the layer is vibrating, then communicate to your client what she is creating for herself.

First Layer–*Grounding, Survival, Physical Body*
Color:

Second Layer–*Clairsentience, Desires, Sexuality, Creativity*
Color:

Third Layer - *Power, Will Power, Energy, Motivation*
Color:

Fourth Layer - *Affinity, Unconditional love*
Color:

Fifth Layer - *Communication*
Color:

Sixth Layer - *How she sees the world*
Color:

Seventh Layer - *How the world sees her*
Color:

Questions
Allow your client to ask you a few questions of her own.

Question:

Question:

Question: